WITHDRAWN

BEAU NASH
*Monarch of Bath
and
Tunbridge Wells*

By

Willard Connely

THE REIGN OF BEAU BRUMMELL

COUNT D'ORSAY

THE TRUE CHESTERFIELD

BEAU NASH

SIR RICHARD STEELE

BRAWNY WYCHERLEY

YOUNG GEORGE FARQUHAR

Richard Nash Esq.r
From an Original painted by Mr. Hoare, and presented to the Corporation of the City of Bath.

Frontispiece

BEAU NASH

MONARCH of BATH and TUNBRIDGE WELLS

by

WILLARD CONNELY

WERNER LAURIE
LONDON

First published in 1955
by T. Werner Laurie Limited
1 *Doughty Street London WC*1
Printed and bound in Great Britain by
The Pitman Press Bath

PRINTED IN GREAT BRITAIN

DA
483
N2
C6

(R 8089)

To
OWEN BROOKE RHOADS

and

EMILY RHOADS

who

upon a day in June

were at

Whitegates

CONTENTS

I	Carmarthen to Oxford	1
II	The Count of Inner Temple	11
III	Bath Discovered	22
IV	A Few Reforms	28
V	Men of Letters	37
VI	A Postal-Clerk	53
VII	Noble Visitors	64
VIII	The Gaming-Table	77
IX	John Wood	86
X	A Curiosity from Holland	94
XI	On the Parade	102
XII	The Prince of Wales	111
XIII	EO	119
XIV	The Great Hospital	129
XV	Decline	137
XVI	Nash and the Novelists	146
XVII	Octogenarian	157
XVIII	The Final Pageant	167
	Notes	175
	Index	181

ILLUSTRATIONS

BEAU NASH	*Frontispiece*
THE KING'S BATH	40
A MINUET	41
QUEEN SQUARE	56
BEAU NASH'S HOUSE	57
THE PRINCE AND PRINCESS OF WALES	72
SARAH PORTER	73
THE GREAT HOSPITAL	88
THE PANTILES, TUNBRIDGE WELLS	89
RALPH ALLEN	152
HENRY FIELDING	153
JAMES QUIN	168
THE ABBEY CHURCH	169

ACKNOWLEDGMENT

The Author and Publishers wish to thank the Corporation of the City of Bath for their kind permission to reproduce 'Beau Nash', 'The King's Bath', 'A Minuet', 'Queen Square', 'Beau Nash's House', and 'Ralph Allen'.

The portrait of Henry Fielding is reproduced by kind permission of the National Portrait Gallery and that of James Quin by courtesy of the Trustees of the Tate Gallery, London.

Acknowledgment is also due to the Tunbridge Wells Museum for the portrait of Sarah Porter, to Baron Studios for the portraits of the Prince and Princess of Wales, reproduced from the originals in Warwick Castle, and to A. F. Kersting for the photograph of the Abbey Church, Bath.

CHAPTER ONE

CARMARTHEN TO OXFORD

WHEN a young man of the name of Nash came out of Haverford West and married ten miles away into the family of Poyer, in Pembroke, he thought he did very well for himself—at least socially. The Nashes were 'known' in the countryside; but the Poyers were of gentler blood. Yet it was not the parents of the bride by whom she herself was most readily identified: she was 'niece to Colonel Poyer'.

At the time of the rising of Oliver Cromwell, the Mayor of Pembroke, who was 'a leading Presbyterian', was John Poyer. For six years Poyer fought to defend Parliament, subduing towns, capturing castles, putting the Royalists to flight. But he received no reimbursement either for himself or for his troops. He is said to have spent £8,000 of his own funds in the cause. In 1648, that loss having remained ignored, Poyer in retaliation seized Pembroke Castle and declared for the King.

Parliament sent Cromwell to attack the turncoat Colonel. Poyer boasted 'he would be the first to charge against Ironsides, whom, though with back of steel and breast of iron, he durst and would encounter'. No such trial of glory seized the imagination of Cromwell. Unromantically he cut off Poyer's water supply, and the Colonel, together with his kinsman David Poyer and several lieutenants, surrendered the Castle.

These men were taken to London and imprisoned. In April 1649, a child drew lots to determine which of the leaders should die. A blank fell to John Poyer. He was executed in Covent Garden.

Richard Nash, then, allied himself with a family whose fortunes had shrunk, at least in Pembroke. One of the family, his bride's aunt Elizabeth Poyer, widow of the Colonel, was impoverished. Yet this family retained their prominence. The late John Poyer, for all his changing of sides, was in the years of the Restoration remembered as an intrepid soldier, an able executive, and a martyr. Nash by his marriage had won distinction if not independence; it remained to be seen whether he should prosper on his own account.

Neither in Pembroke nor in Haverford West did he get on. The Nash family were not in commerce; Richard Nash had not grown up attuned to 'trade'; and in his earliest attempts at it, after his marriage, he failed. The question was whither to go in order to try afresh. He and his wife pitched upon Swansea, some fifty miles east of Haverford, possibly because other Poyers were there living more comfortably. Amongst them were Matthew Poyer and his family, also Hannah and Catherine Poyer. In South Wales the clan of Poyer were people of mark.

It was probably in about 1670 that the Nashes settled in Swansea. They took a small house at the corner of College and Goat Streets. In the course of making acquaintance in the town, Nash met one John Man, who was engaged 'in the trade of glasseworke'. One of his chief products was quart-bottles, mottled, toward the moulding of which his equipment included 'working-tools, potts, utensils, sands, ashes, kilpes (hooks), and such-like materials'. The simplicity sounded to Nash like something for nothing. To make so staple an article as quart-bottles, to all appearances for the convenient apportionment and marketing of a commodity no less in demand, apparently appealed to him. And he liked John Man. Nash bought a 'minor' partnership in the factory.

By virtue of entering business he became a burgess, or

freeman, of Swansea. This designation carried its privileges, but also its restrictions; for example, burgesses were obliged to 'trade' with freemen only, and not with sencers, or 'un-freemen', who formed a large constituency of the local population.

These sencers, themselves denied the right to engage in trade or business without special permission, furtively often did so, selling at a lower price things that were in short supply. To the temptation of a certain sencer, 'Mr Nash', early in 1674, gave way, and made bold to buy 'a parcel of salt'. He was detected, and fined, as recorded in the Common Hall Books.

The income of the Nashes from the 'glasseworke' was small, because the capacity of the factory was small, something under 1,000 bottles a week. Nor was their livelihood made any easier when in the autumn of this year, in the house in Goat Street, Nash's wife lay in. On 18 October she bore a son. Three weeks later, 7 November, the infant was christened in Swansea Parish Church, and named for his father, Richard.

It is possible that by 1677 Nash was able to claim a larger share of the profits from bottles, since in that year John Man was appointed Collector of the Port of Swansea. This post must frequently have detained him at a distance from the factory, with the result that the responsibilities of Nash would increase. And Nash lived near enough to superintend at all times. The site of the 'glassehouse' was now in the Strand, only 300 yards from Goat Street.

Of little Richard Nash, the small boy, the heir to whatever the inheritance from his parents was worth, nothing is known except his 'natural vivacity'. He had a long face, and a long narrow nose growing aquiline. His mouth was small; but the lips were sensuous, the lower one slightly protruding. In his chin he had a dimple. His eyes, almost bovine, seemed to be wells of fun; it was in them, rather than from his mouth, that his smile began.

When he was twelve years old, in 1686, he left the

scene of his childhood—dominated, for him, by his birthplace at one end of the street and by the ancient castle of the Dukes of Beaufort at the other—to 'learn his lessons' more formally at Carmarthen, twenty miles to the north.

It would be agreeable to think that his father had so far prospered that this expense was no hardship, to think that Nash Point, the eastern boundary of Swansea, had accordingly been named for the burgess Richard Nash. More probable is it that the landmark was so-called after John Nash (no evident kin), Receiver-General of South Wales under the present King James II. John Nash was at the moment unjustly returning many persons in the country to be in arrears to the Crown. If the name of Nash was doubly known in Swansea, in neither case did it stand for very solid achievement.

Young Richard's father no doubt chose for his son the Free Grammar School of Queen Elizabeth, in Carmarthen, partly because from its proximity it was the school he could best afford. One approached Carmarthen, in the foothills of Bryn Merthyn, by crossing the ancient stone bridge over the Towy, like Cromwell, and winding up a serpentine road to Castle Green. Not far beyond, in Priory Street, stood the school. The Great Queen, as a loyal Welsh woman, had founded it by decree in 1576, for the 'education and instruction of boys and youths in grammar and other inferior books'. As she unfortunately did not maintain it so well, the Bishop of Llandaff, under the Commonwealth, left the school £20 a year. Subsequently local men had made other bequests, the most recent of which, in 1676, was a house and land adjacent, willed to the school by William Jones, Archdeacon of Carmarthen. This house was now used for the Headmaster's lodge.

The school presented no door to the street, but three large square windows with leaded panes, and above them, smaller gabled windows. Arms of the school, a castle and a lion ambulant, graced the middle gable, with scrolls overall, and from the peak a wrought weather vane. The ornaments above the other gables, and at either end of the peak of the roof, took the form of inverted turnips. On the other side of the house the door to the school opened upon a playing-field, while the three leaded windows on this side, high up to prevent the boys from looking out, bore the odd shape of slices of bread cut lengthwise. Along the street, to the left, ran a high wall of stone. The Headmaster's house, at the right, was a building quite as substantial as the school and a little higher; it was set far enough back from the pavement to afford space for a narrow garden, itself protected by an iron fence.

It so happened that the arrival of young Nash coincided with the arrival of a new Headmaster, John Maddocks, of Llandaff. He was a bachelor of thirty, had taken his degree at Jesus College, Oxford, and had been a master at Abergwilly. Under this gentleman R. Nash settled into his work, alongside H. Jones, T. Powell, and other worthy Welsh boys of the vicinity.

For five years Richard immured himself within Carmarthen School. While he is not known to have taken any prizes or honours in point of scholarship, he did develop physically. In later youth he distinguished himself as a standing-jumper, both forward and backward; it is likely that upon the playing-field of the school young Nash first grew aware of the springiness peculiar to his considerable length of leg.

From the Headmaster, Richard could scarcely have avoided hearing a good deal about Jesus College. He was eager for Oxford, chiefly on the ground that it meant release; he wanted to be 'grown up'. Nor was his father a man to discourage him, although family funds were not very abundant. By early 1692 the manager of the bottle-factory had withdrawn from his 'glassehouse', departed from Swansea, and returned with his family to live in Pembroke. Whether he retired from business altogether, or took up in Pembroke a different means of livelihood, does not appear. If from his venture in Swansea he lost little, neither did he greatly profit, since in sending his son to Oxford the elder Nash entered him in Jesus not as a commoner, but in the lower rank of batteler, a pupil who was to pay only for what he ordered.

It was on 19 March 1692 that Richard as a lad of seventeen matriculated; the status of his father was designated *pleb*. Four other pupils, oddly assorted, joined Jesus College at the same time: from Wales (Dyserth, Flintshire), David Powell, who was twenty-one years old; John Hill, son of a gentleman who was well-to-do; Lewis Hill, also a gentleman's son, but not so well off; and James Lake, a pupil of about Nash's age, but a commoner. Lake was the son and namesake of the Reverend James Lake of Black Torrington, Devon, a man who was prepared to let the battels of his heir run up in Jesus College without stint. Whatever these other pupils were to do, Richard Nash was there to read law if he would.

The college, instituted only about a century earlier by Dr Hugh Price, a butcher's son of Brecon, and called 'Queen Elizabeth's foundation', was still in process of being built. It had its quadrangle, with gabled windows all round; but a second or inner quadrangle showed completed only one side, jutting out to form a T, and about half of the side opposite. The rest of the east and north sides stood quite open. Work upon this inner square—of grey stone like the original one—had been going on for fifteen years; in 1683, when aided by a gift from a recent Principal, Sir Leoline Jenkins, the Fellows had put up a library, with a Common Room beneath it, the Duke and Duchess of York, with their daughter Princess Anne, had come to 'view Sir Leoline's new buildings'. Jenkins died two years later, and although he made the college his heir, in the amount of £700 a year, he also left the place encumbered with 'old and desperate debts'. This burden it was that slowed up the building.

At the time of the arrival of young Nash, the Principal

was Jonathan Edwards of Wrexham, aged about fifty-five. He had begun as a servitor in Christ Church. Edwards was a thrifty man; although during the Monmouth Rebellion in 1685 he had lent his horses to the university troop, he collected 23 shillings for their oats. As Richard Nash joined the College its Principal, bent upon renovating its chapel, was selling the old altar-rails to the Rector of Lincoln for £3. Anti-Calvinists said Edwards was 'not a man of the great integrity he should have been'. Yet within his means he was a benefactor of both the chapel and the library. He loved controversy, but remained unaware that spasms of gastric gout sharpened his polemics. The one upon which he was engaged when Nash and his fellow-freshmen first met him bore this resounding title: 'Preservation against Socinianism, that doctrine which taught denial of the Trinity, personality of the devil, depravity of man, vicarious atonement, and eternal punishment'.

Like his predecessor Sir Leoline, Edwards was a donor of books to the library, but on a more modest scale. The gift from Jenkins comprehended theology, classics, history, and in particular canon and civil law, a gift almost rivalling that of Lord Herbert of Cherbury a generation earlier, Herbert whose bequest embraced 'practically the whole range of learning of the day'. The entire catalogue of the library, in case young Nash might be tempted to look at it, made a list of about 2,000 volumes. Principal Edwards was hardly a man to drive such a pupil to read.

If his record at Carmarthen School was any guide, Nash was oftener to be seen in hall. Apart from its high table, on which reposed a Charles II bowl, weight $4\frac{1}{4}$ pounds, a magnificent porringer of the same period, and a one-gallon tankard of the time of James II, hall contained one long table for bachelors and commoners, and one table for demi-commoners, as batelers were otherwise probably called. Portraits in possession of the college were those of its original benefactor Hugh Price, of Queen Elizabeth, of Charles I and Charles II. An oriel window bowed out to the left of high table, while round the hall ran 'a wainscot curiously graven'.

About two-thirds of the pupils were Welsh, the rest English. The batteler from Pembroke was not prejudiced. If he meant James Lake when in after years he spoke of a college-mate who was reading divinity, who was 'rich as the devil', and who lived in Devonshire, one of Nash's first companions was English. Of himself and of the man in question Nash asserted that 'we both studied damnationly hard'. However, undergraduates in Oxford were in those days far freer than at present to come and go as they pleased.

Richard Nash is said to have brought into the college a fiddle, to save him from overtaxing his brain, even from attending too many 'public or private lectures'. This sounds as if he avoided tutor and professors alike, evidently not a difficult thing to do, inasmuch as there is in the College archives no record either of lectures being given or of classes being held in the College, whether by Fellows of Jesus or by Fellows from other Colleges. Nash during his ample hours of leisure was able to resort freely to his 'tobacco-box', another of the amenities which he reputedly kept in his rooms. In athletics, he no doubt practised his speciality: a bit given to hyperbole, he later insisted that he 'could once leap forty-two feet upon level ground, at three standing jumps'.

Compared with some of his contemporaries, such as James Lake or John Hill, who had more money to spend and in consequence battelled five or six pounds a term, Nash was not extravagant. He was mindful of his father's small means, and kept down to a little over three pounds. The question of how much he spent outside College is another matter. Before the autumn, before Michaelmas term, he grew involved with the young women of Oxford, 'girls with some beauty, some coquetry, and little fortune', who were in the habit of lying in wait for the more amorous members of the university. This diversion was rather expensive.

For all that, young Nash seems to have reserved some of his time, if it was not often given to his heavy books of law, to try his hand at writing in the current fashion a play or two. The star of Restoration comedy was still in the ascendant; although Sir George Etherege had just died, and although Wycherley was no longer writing, Dryden was not quite done, and the plays of all of them were still being revived and applauded. From their echoes, Richard Nash in Oxford was not too far distant.

Through the winter he stayed on in Jesus College. By this time he had fallen into a 'dozen delicate dilemmas' with the coquettes. His mistake, so the story goes, was that he let one of them, a woman 'disproportioned in age', and called by the censorious 'a trull of wit and beauty', lure him into an entanglement. It is said that Nash was actually on the point of marrying this siren, who at any rate was one of those 'of little fortune'.

The moral tutor of the victim, or some such person in authority at the College, heard of the alliance impending, and took alarm. There seemed to be no safe way of dealing with the crisis but to send the errant pupil down. Nash had in any case already demonstrated, after four terms in Oxford, terms of endeavour no more studious than fiddling, play-writing, and philandering, that he would be no loss to the profession of law. It was perhaps sufficiently wise to warn his father in distant Pembroke. The elder Nash might well take measures, at least for the immediate future, to control his son's erotic impulses.

After March 1693 this pupil paid no more battels. He had been up just a year. During his first term, or quarter, when the novelty of Jesus College kept him reasonably within its walls, his battels, chiefly for food, made a total of £3 16s. 10d. In the summer quarter this amount dropped to £3 2s. 9d. In the autumn, by which time the local ladies were seeing to it that Mr Nash did not waste too much of his time in college, these battels dropped to only £2 15s. 7d. However, the chill of winter, if not a degree of caution in ardency, seems to have turned him more indoors once again: he ended his fourth term with a payment of £3 9s. 10d.

A rumour has persisted that Nash left Oxford owing money to his College, and that this liability stood against his name on the College books. But in the list of those whose battels were unpaid his name does not appear, and it may therefore be assumed that he quitted the portals of Jesus all clear. Nevertheless Richard Nash evidently departed in some haste, or as if for one reason or another he had been a little distracted in packing up. It is conceivable that the 'trull', who was supposed to have 'turned his brain', stood on the watch for him, possibly lurking near the gates, and that her impetuous undergraduate had by devious means to elude her. At all events he left behind a pair of boots (these, it is true, he might have knowingly discarded), together with certain belongings, dear to his idling hours, that only an obsession with his *inamorata* could have caused him to overlook. In his vacated room were found his violin, his tobacco-box, and two manuscripts of plays with which Richard Nash had intended to reinvigorate the theatre of London.

CHAPTER TWO

THE COUNT OF INNER TEMPLE

IN Pembroke the elder Nash pondered upon the crisis. Concluding that he might do worse for his son than to supplant the laxity of Oxford by the chastening of the Army, he bought young Richard a pair of colours, which entitled him to an ensigncy in the Guards.

The new officer, smart in his uniform, joined his regiment in London in this same year of 1693. If his father was again assuming for him a risk in respect of the wiles of women, the risk in London was better worth taking, because the Army, in particular a Guards regiment, was an introduction to society.

The regiment turned out to be nothing else. Richard Nash in his scarlet coat cut a striking figure not so much on parade, but in the drawing-rooms. At drill he objected to being subordinate; he did not fancy reproof; and when social engagements of promise beckoned him elsewhere he found his presence with the Guards irksome if not downright frivolous. Growing aware that he was as attractive to the ladies of London as he had been to the rustic adventuresses of Oxford, he 'put his whole intellect into a bow'. But when, to enhance his desirability, he vowed to dress in the topmost fashion, he discovered that his pay as an ensign hardly met the demands of his tailor. Sly rumour had it that in order to close the gap Nash held up 'fat graziers and pursy parsons' on Hounslow Heath.

This would not do, for long. Nor did the Army detain him beyond the year. The one way to reconcile his father to another change of career was to revert to the study of law, the calling out of which the glassmaker had expected eventual recompense for his son's education. Law, declared young Nash, could best be pursued at the Inner Temple. His father apparently did not demur, and Richard sold his commission to enable him to enter his name in 1694 upon the Temple books.

The Templar of the day was a modification of the rake at the court of Charles II. Wit, playgoer, critic, epicure, deferred to in conversation, the Templar was held to be a judge of taste, of jesting, of the limits of eccentric behaviour. If he lived too near the city to be completely the man of fashion, he lived too far from commerce to be dyed with business; but whenever he strayed into either sphere, he knew what to do. In society the Templar, with his embroidered coat and his sword, usually outpaced the soldier, three assets being assumed: assurance, readiness of speech, and the art of living without money. Richard Nash, full of confidence, believed himself at the age of twenty qualified to rise in this milieu.

The London of William and Mary offered ample opportunity for his forays outside the Temple gates. It was a London of taverns and coffee-houses, of fencing, duelling, and cock-fighting, of morning calls in the bedchamber and assignations at sundown in the park, of lords and ladies taking tea at ten and not often heeding church bells at eleven, of chairs carried of a morning through the narrow lanes or of afternoon coaches spinning round Hyde Park, of promenades in Covent Garden most inviting to 'young gentlemen from the university'; but above all, it was a gambling London. Nash made the valuable discovery that at the gaming-table, whether in the Temple or elsewhere, he possessed a manner. Upon it he reckoned to defray his expenses.

In ruffles and velvet coat, in diamond brooch and diamond buckles, this uncommon young Templar drew friends to his side by his very dress. In addition, he was blessed with 'the spirit of frolic', as his fiddle at Oxford had evinced without earning him much honour therefor; in London this spirit endeared him to all those—ever a considerable proportion—who themselves lacked truly amiable qualities. He cultivated young worldlings of rank and wealth, with whom, at the theatre, he exhibited himself in the side-boxes. Of law he read no more than he had done in Jesus College; there were too many drawing-rooms crying for his presence to make them 'complete', rooms which he both graced and quickened. Nash was known to be poor. Yet he was always 'fine'. At games of chance his winnings so consistently exceeded his losses that it almost seemed as if some of his friends who were well-to-do let him win, now and again, lest they be deprived of his elegance. Round the Inns of Court Richard Nash, singled out as a character, gained a sobriquet: they called him 'the Count'.

It was a coincidence that the year 1695 was not only the year of Nash's coming of age, but the year which, upon the death of Queen Mary, witnessed the single accession of William to the throne. Nash was accorded the chance to celebrate both occasions in one. The benchers, after their custom, were staging a pageant in honour of the King, and in view of the capacity for leadership now so evident in Nash, they elected him Master of the Revels. Here was a young man, his associates considered, who seemed able instinctively to pronounce upon questions of decorum, of regularity. He could be relied upon for precision and smoothness in the smallest details, the sum of which, after all, might make or mar an entertainment in the eyes of exacting royalty.

There is no record of the programme incidental to this exhibition. But in an age of resplendent costume even upon occasions that were not extraordinary, one can imagine the gold and the lace, the velvet and the sequins, bearing upon history both past and current, in the parade produced by the Count. As impresario he won the day.

William III was charmed by this performance brought off with such finish by a man less than half his own years.

Disregarding the youth of the director, the King offered him a knighthood.

Nash hesitated. Though he always appeared to be a personage well above want, he still had no assured private means, as those to whom his personal expenses were due were only too well aware. To his sovereign he therefore ventured to reply with a proviso:

'Please your Majesty, if you intend to make me a knight, I wish it may be one of your poor (military) knights of Windsor, and then I shall have a fortune at least able to support my title.'

Here the question of age, not to mention service on the field of battle, created a difficulty, especially in the mind of a soldier-king. Nash no doubt anticipated that it would. He heard nothing more of his knighthood. And he was quite content to remain a 'Count'.

The wider fame which he enjoyed from the pageant did not always earn him notice so flattering. He was now acquainted with officers as well in the Navy as in the Army, and soon after the revels a number of naval men invited him aboard ship for a merry evening. His hosts neglected to inform Nash that their ship was under immediate orders to sail for the Mediterranean, and toward the end of a highly bibulous night their guest made his way to a welcome bunk. In the course of the next day he awakened to find himself 'shanghaied'. Far out at sea, there was no turning back. But it is not a matter of record that the Count grieved over the cruise, the holiday after his manifold exertions in the Temple.

Nor did this escapade do him any harm with his fellow-benchers. Nash brought back a story that the ship had run into an exchange of shots with a hostile vessel, that his 'friend', the man chiefly responsible for kidnapping him, had been killed fighting alongside him, and that he himself was carrying in his leg a souvenir of the battle. (He had not achieved a limp.) But whatever the benchers thought of this yarn, they proceeded to elect the Count their treasurer. They knew he was a gamester;

this they accepted, believing him to be an honest and a generous one.

In this office Nash to his personal relief was allowed an expense account, subject to the scrutiny of the officers of the society. He knew how to spend, even when the money 'came easily'. To spend was not always to buy, tangibly. There was a form of spending from the heart; if this at the same time enhanced a man's reputation, well and good. One day, as he was walking through the cloister, the new treasurer overheard one poor man say to another:

'Such a small sum would make me the happiest man in the world.'

Nash privately enquired into the character of this man, who was speaking of the benefits that the amount of ten pounds would bring him. The report was that charity for him would not be amiss. From the coffers of the Temple the compassionate treasurer took the money and sent it him.

This item was unknown. But since Nash in his grand manner was also making a number of unusual and noticeable disbursements, the society grew alarmed, and ordered a committee to investigate the management of their treasury. At length this committee appeared before the Templars assembled, to read out their findings, a statement which included a recital of the articles purchased.

If the benchers expected to hear in the manipulations of the Count a degree of originality, they were perhaps less prepared for daring, in particular the daring of charity. A committeeman recited the item, 'For making a man happy, ten pounds'. With no further ado at all, the house passed the accounts of Richard Nash.

Preoccupied with the benchers in term, and with the gamblers from Aix and Spa who infested London throughout the winter, Nash allotted to the ladies more of his time in the softer months. He continued no less susceptible to the company of women than in Oxford, and in the season of 1696 he singled out Miss Verdun, the beautiful daughter of a parvenu, to marry. Her father, delighted that a cynosure of the nobility like 'Mr Nash' should condescend to such a match, put all the energy of a man recently rich into favouring the proposal. But with the young lady herself the case proved not very plain sailing. She repulsed both her suitor and her father. When Nash went to her, she bluntly told him she intended to marry another man; and when her father insisted she accept Nash, she flouted old Verdun's commands as if her choice were none of his concern.

It was then that the Count did the unexpected, made his increasingly characteristic though ever unpredictable change of course. He returned to the baffled father, whom he persuaded to let the girl marry the man she preferred. Not only so; he amiably confronted Miss Verdun and begged her to send for his rival. To them both he then gave his blessing. This was but another form of the 'generosity' which Nash had displayed toward the poor man in the cloister.

So often did the tale of this contretemps between Nash and Miss Verdun enliven the coffee-houses frequented by the wits that its situations, suggesting at several points the stuff of drama, did not go long unpondered. Before the very year was out, Captain John Vanbrugh pitched upon the story. He had just brought mirth to Drury Lane with his comedy *The Relapse*; this he was now following up with an adaptation from the French, a language for which even a late detention in the Bastille had not reduced his zest. The play in hand was *Esope à la Ville*, written in 1690 by Edmé Boursault, who designed that Aesop appear in each scene and recite a fable. Vanbrugh thought this scheme hardly dramatic enough, and certainly not overcharged with comedy. Refashioning the play, which he entitled simply *Aesop*, he confessed 'I have wholly added the fifth act'. That act, topical enough, he made out of the Nash-Verdun affair.

Vanbrugh was a swift workman in the theatre. It had taken him only six weeks to write *The Relapse*, which with Colley Cibber as Lord Foppington he had presented as recently as Boxing Day 1696, and now in January he had *Aesop* ready, again for Cibber, who took the title part. While there is no evidence that either Cibber or Vanbrugh was personally acquainted with Nash, the character of Aesop, a beau, at least as he comported himself in Act V, was the Count of Inner Temple in the course of his involvement with Miss Verdun. She herself appeared as Euphronia, enacted by Mrs Temple, with a foil in the person of Doris, her nurse, really a more important part, which was assigned to the witty Susannah Verbruggen. The man with whom Miss Verdun was actually in love was seen as Oronces, played by Mr Harland, while her father, old Verdun, emerged as Learchus, a figure similar in character and undertaken by Cibber's friend Thomas Doggett. In the frame of the play Learchus was governor of the community in which the action occurred. Another significant item in the *dramatis personae* read 'People who come to Aesop, upon several occasions, independent one of another'. So they had for several years come to Richard Nash, upon divers errands, during his unique membership in the Inner Temple.

The materials of the Nash-Verdun episode fell neatly enough into the shaping fingers of John Vanbrugh. Euphronia, in a disputatious scene with her nurse Doris, and reluctant to heed the matrimonial bidding of her father the parvenu, found it 'hard to think Aesop a beau'. But the heroine feared that if she disobliged her parent he would give her portion to her younger sister. Euphronia might be driven into the match; in that case, she was 'relying on the natural inconstancy of her sex, and on woman's contradiction'. In the face of these expostulations Doris the confidante took an independent view: she urged Euphronia to run away, even with a penniless man, if she loved him.

Aesop then entered, to hear from Euphronia that she was already in love (with Oronces), and had been so for two years past. But Aesop considered this merely a whim, and to show what he thought of a lover content to wait all that time, he said 'We'll be married tomorrow'. As Euphronia was pleading for a stay of a few days, her father appeared and commanded her to marry Aesop 'this instant'. Whereat Oronces joined the fray; he begged them to 'wait until tomorrow'. Aesop having airily withdrawn from the scene, the impatient Learchus burst out, 'If Aesop's my son-in-law he'll make me a lord!'

This was too much for Oronces. He threatened the old man. Learchus, as governor, straightway had Oronces gaoled. 'I'm father-in-law', then cried Learchus, 'to the great Aesop'. And at this point a musician who was present to take part in the impending ceremony assumed the part of Cassandra: 'Learchus will turn fool, and Euphronia will turn strumpet'.

Aesop meantime had concluded that the wedding was to proceed. Arriving, he insisted upon the release of his rival Oronces, whom he wished invited to the ceremony as a witness. As soon as all was ready, and they were standing before the priest, Aesop asked for Euphronia's hand, which Learchus had to give to him. Whilst the priest was pronouncing the last line, Aesop adroitly joined the hands of Euphronia and Oronces. 'A tyrant to his children', observed Aesop, 'is fit to govern nobody but himself'. But there was only one thought persisting in the mind of Learchus, who said, 'I shall be a great man'.

As Euphronia had got Oronces, and not Aesop, so had Miss Verdun got the man of her choice, and not Nash. Yet the aftermath of the Verdun wedding proved every way unhappy for the bridegroom. Miss Verdun, until her father had grown suddenly rich, had been more at ease in the company of a level considerably lower than that of either her husband or Richard Nash. In the spring of 1697 she eloped with her footman. How many who had seen the play *Aesop* recalled the advice of Doris to Euphronia: 'to run away, even with a penniless man, if she loved him'? Probably as many as those who also remembered the words of the musician: 'Learchus will turn fool and Euphronia will turn strumpet'.

When Nash heard the news of the actual elopement, he gave a gay party at the Smyrna Coffee-house in Pall Mall. One 'received acquaintance' at the Smyrna, purged body with tea and brain with snuff, then argued. From the seat of learning in the left chimney-corner Nash addressed his guests. 'Gentlemen', said he, 'virtue is its own reward'.

The comedy *Aesop* had enjoyed no run. But it would hardly have yielded even a benefit performance for its author had he not interpolated the story about which the town had been talking from Temple Bar to Haymarket. Cibber delighted in his part of Aesop, in particular because at the end he wore fine feathers, like Nash himself. The comedian gained no little satisfaction from having been 'equally approved' in the part of Aesop, as he had been in Lord Foppington. He was said to have acted Aesop 'with that easy gravity which becomes the man who instructs by fable'. Likewise, easy gravity was a trait which had for some years been developing in the Count of Inner Temple.

In the event, Vanbrugh's loss—compared with his success from *The Relapse*—turned out to be Nash's gain. While Vanbrugh appeared to be a dubious judge of a play worth adapting, Nash upon this dramatization of his own experience was regarded as a man astute in his relations with women. At least he had learned to be a cautious suitor.

Out of such encounters others grew, as if proliferating. To a friend, the Count once showed twenty love-letters, his post for one day, some of the letters containing money. It explained in no small part how he lived. By the turn of the century the pursuit of law was virtually out of his reckoning. The two things he pursued were society, hinged upon women, and gambling, hinged upon the continental professionals who made London their winter quarters. Sometimes in warmer weather he took a northward excursion to the gaming-table, stopping with a few companions at York, probably as a 'base' for operations at Scarborough. It was the young gamester's first sight of a watering-place. As this shift of emphasis in Nash's outlook upon a career became more marked, so did his absences from the Inns of Court. He took lodgings in Berkeley Square, an address more convenient to the drawing-rooms of the ladies who sought after him.

Yet the Count had friends both sober and serious. One was young Samuel Clarke, metaphysicist, disciple of Newton, and Chaplain to the Bishop of Norwich. (Clarke was soon to find renown as vicar of St. James's, Piccadilly.) Upon a certain day Nash set forth to visit him. Clarke at the time was miraculously extracting mirth and laughter from a philosophic discussion with the elderly John Locke, and two or three others of suspended gravity. Chancing to look from the window, the host descried Nash bearing toward the house, 'Boys, boys!' Clarke exclaimed, 'let us now be wise, for here is a fool coming'. It was their jester, only with sword and ruffles instead of cap and bells, and he was welcome.

But if Nash was now fading away from the Temple, he was not cutting adrift from all his friends round Temple Bar. One night he supped late with one of them who lived in that vicinity. Upon leaving, the Count called a hackney-coach to carry him to Berkeley Square.

'I'd be glad sir', said the driver, who knew him, 'to drive you to hell'.

'Then', replied Nash, 'you must go in first yourself'.

The rejoinder was as quick then as now: 'No; I'd back you in'.

These days in Berkeley Square, however, were not to be prolonged indefinitely, even though the Count as a personage so distinguished that Square. Arrived at the age of thirty, in 1704, he 'found his mind superior to both the army and the law'. After his twelve years of experience in London, he knew he was destined for leadership, but without being a general; for governing, but without being a judge. Was there such a thing as leadership in gambling? If there was Richard Nash had not risen to it in London. His hold upon play was ever precarious; for all his suavity, the continental sharpers pressed him hard, and so did some of the native gamesters as well.

Nash noticed that not all of the foreign players were now migrating to Aix or Spa for the summer. A certain number of them, and of the English too, were going down to Bath. But did a visit to Bath promise much different from that excursion to York, to Scarborough? There he had lost a sizable sum, and had to borrow fifty pounds from a man he had known in Jesus College. What was Bath but a den of cripples? Why should a 'healthy gambler' try to take away their money? Did they in any case have enough worth winning?

But in the two years last past Queen Anne and Prince George had spent September in Bath. In consequence, visitors other than the infirm, visitors also of standing, were now doing likewise. They were people with money to stake, they could afford to gamble; and the gamesters of London and Europe had lost no time in finding it out. Nash himself had not hurried to join the pack. But in 1705, having nothing better to do in London, he accompanied a few confident young men down to Bath, for a thrust at cards and hazard.

CHAPTER THREE

BATH DISCOVERED

AS Richard Nash passed through the North Gate of Bath, an arch fifteen feet high with two posterns for pedestrians, the 'Triumphal Arch of the City' through which Queen Anne and the Prince had entered in pomp, conducted by 'a regiment of Bathonian soldiers and two hundred Amazons', he trod territory whose overlordship was identified with the scene of his boyhood. The first Duke of Beaufort, whose seat was at Badminton, only fourteen miles away, had not only been patron of Bath until his death in 1700; he had leased Beaufort Castle, the landmark of Swansea, for a 'glasseworke', and from 1687 the Castle had been so operated by John Man, whose partner was Nash's father. Wherefore the younger Nash, upon arriving in Bath as the son of an occupier of Beaufort Castle, need not have felt utterly an outsider.

The second Duke, grandson of the first, was now only twenty-one. Although he was in the habit of coming over to Bath for pleasure, he did not keep up his grandfather's interest in expanding the town into something more than a health resort. The old Duke had laid out a bowling-green, sanctioned gambling in the town-hall, and opened the town-hall to dancing, instead of requiring the dances to be held outdoors. This indoor dancing, however, had hardly depopulated the adjacent gambling-rooms; ten couples on the floor were thought to be a considerable assembly. A manager of all was nevertheless believed advisable, and to this office Beaufort had appointed a

Captain Webster, whom he regarded as 'gallant and ceremonious'.

Webster was a local man, and he dressed like one. He wore a square-cut coat, 'a vast neckerchief tied in a vast bow', and dark breeches stuffed into top-boots. Of middle size, he was a figure of 'spirit and address', with a 'thirst' for gaming, also with a thirst. At the dances, which he was accustomed to attend encouraged by a few drinks, he had a way of bringing his feet down as if to crush his enemies with his boot-heels.

The boots of Captain Webster, as Master of Ceremonies, rather set the tone of Bath. While the Court had periodically come down for the waters since Restoration times, from Barbara Villiers and Louise de Querouaille to Queen Mary of Modena, and while the visits of Queen Anne had led to a more sustained summer incursion of the nobility, a cleavage between the persons of title and the 'lower gentry' of means kept the social life of the town out of joint. The middle classes aspired to the gaieties hitherto confined to the nobility. But since this lesser breed were uncouth, the lords and ladies now coming to Bath in the wake of the Queen kept aloof, and as a rule let the others dance by themselves. In the town-hall Webster permitted boots, like his own; he also allowed the men to smoke and the women to wear aprons. A duchess or a countess who for a lark went in for vulgarity joined in the dancing; but the majority stopped in their lodgings, and that was the reason the assemblies in the town-hall seldom ran to more than ten couples. Even so, all of the lodgings were threadbare and exorbitant, the chair-men insulting, the dining-rooms mean and dingy, and the pump-house without a director.

Nash had not come to Bath to criticise these things, but to replenish his purse. He met Webster, who is said to have 'received him with great politeness and particular marks of respect'. The repute of a man who had so successfully staged a pageant for the late King must have reached far outside of London. And Nash visited the town-hall to which Webster had at least transferred the dancing, put it under a roof, instead of letting it continue haphazard on the bowling-green. The man from the Temple found this town-hall a well-proportioned block of a building, with four columns gracing its two upper floors, and surmounted by a statue of a goddess holding sword and branch. To try his luck beneath this auspicious goddess, he went in, and in impassive metropolitan style began to gamble.

For seven weeks, the extent, at this time, of the season in Bath, Nash raked in over a hundred pounds a week. It was enough to give him a very good opinion of Bath, and enough to give Webster an equally good opinion of Nash. The two men became friendly. Well before the season closed, Webster appointed Richard Nash his colleague, his chief of staff, finding uses for him, quite apart from the gaming-table, many matters requiring attention between the baths and the pump. The Captain was for one thing building a pump-room, to shelter the waters as he had done the dancing; and this new building needed supervision.

Nash found the local population between two and three thousand only; Bath was neither town nor city. If in the season it was as crowded as London, for the rest of the year it was as desolate as a wilderness, and 'its chiefest inhabitants turnspit dogs'. Now, with sojourners on every side, Webster's assistant took stock of them, and of what they did. In the forenoon the rendezvous was the Coffee-house, where at 10 o'clock 'fools, cullies, squires, beaux and critics' assembled. They raffled for a guinea; and somebody won a snuffbox worth four. Others took sherry at the Bristol-milk dairy-house. Better company, and good wine as well, could be found at a 'pub' called 'Horrid Tom's'.

It was to these resorts that the invalids came also, after bathing, the baths being open from 6 to 9 a.m. The largest and hottest (103 degrees) was the King's Bath, near the southwest side of the Abbey church. The bathing was mixed. About fifty persons daily immersed themselves, with about half as many guides. Of the patients, an unsympathetic observer at this time remarked: 'By their scorbutic carcasses and lackered hides you'd think they'd lain pickling a century of years in the Stygian lake'. The guides held up some of the more arthritic cases, while others 'scrubbed their putrified carcasses like a race-horse'. One woman, half-covered with searcloth, had 'more scars than Lazarus, doing penance for the sins of her youth'. At her elbow, this critical watcher noted 'a young hero supported by a couple of guides, racked with aches and intolerable pains, cursing of Middlesex Court and Beveridge's dancing-school as heartily as Job the day of his birth'. This bath was in the open air. It contained niches set in its sides for those who could not bear immersion very long, or who could not stand up in the water for more than a few minutes at a time.

The Queen's Bath, adjoining, was a bit cooler by reason of being supplied from the overflow of the larger one, while the 'Hot' Bath, also cooler, and farther away, was only one-eighth the dimensions of the King's. But it was to the Cross Bath, still farther on, so called from a cross erected in the middle of it, that the observer from the King's took his steps. Bordered by a dozen stone arches, 'for menne to stande under in tyme of reyne', the Cross Bath was favoured by the 'gentry'. Here the observer saw 'the spectators in the galleries pleasing their roving fancies with this lady's face, another's eyes, a third's heaving breasts and profound air. In one corner stood an old lecher, no less than three-score and ten, making love to a young lady not exceeding fourteen. Half-tub chairs lined with blankets (bearing the bathers to and fro) plied as thick as coaches at the playhouse'.

Richard Nash, the assistant master of ceremonies, could hardly have failed as he looked upon these scenes to notice the headdress of the women in the water. It was as mediaeval as ever in the time of Louis XI of France, when his Queen and her ladies, in pointed velvet hats bejewelled and hung with lace, invited the fat wives of the bourgeois to vie with them in headdress and bathe, royalty and commoners all together, in the Seine. So at Bath the ladies, in particular the younger and comelier ones, adorned their heads for the waters 'with all the lures of dress that the fashion of the times or their own fancies could furnish'. Part of the equipment of each lady, too, was a floating dish or pan, in which she kept a handkerchief, a snuff-box, and a little bunch of flowers; it was her sail-boat, her argosy, perhaps a restorative against faintness.

As the day wore on the visitors walked in the Grove, an agreeable spot scented with pine, where one could find not only several raffling-shops, but sets of ninepins, 'tipping all nine for a guinea'. Beyond, on the green, there was usually a bowling-match at five o'clock. In the evening the scene of the walk was 'the meadows'. Those who had come to Bath because it was a resort lately patronised by the Queen liked to think of these meadows as 'a second Hyde Park for coaches and a St. James's for beaux and belles'. But they were as likely to find there mantua-makers dandled by fops, antiquated roysterers, blustering bullies and London jilts, bantering young squires and shopkeepers' apprentices. Night-time, really, was the hour awaited by those who had idled all day, by those who had come from town for profit and adventure. The scene was the town-hall, its door kept by two burly beadles, who demanded half a guinea for admission to the ball. The music, furnished by local 'artists', was indifferent; but it was some improvement upon the single fiddle and hautboy that Webster had found playing for the country-dances on the green. Dancers and gamblers alike partook of a supper of sweetmeats and wine, presided over by a 'lady donor' in distinctive costume. Before the 'break-up', all chose her successor, another lady, for the next evening.

On one of these nights Captain Webster, who as a

professional gambler himself was ever at the tables, quarrelled with another gamester over the stakes. Webster claimed a fair win; the loser challenged it. Such altercations were not infrequent, and sometimes ended in compromise; but gentlemen at Bath wore swords, upon whose hilts their hands tended to slap if words ran high. This happened in the case of Webster and his accuser, nor was the situation eased by the likelihood that the Captain, as usual, was somewhat fuddled with wine.

In the Grove, that sweet-scented nook dedicated to nothing more deadly than ninepins and raffles, the two men faced each other, and fought their duel. The challenging gambler ran Webster through the body. He died on the spot.

Immediately it became the duty of the Corporation of Bath to elect a successor to the Captain. Well aware that Richard Nash had for some weeks been effectively assisting Webster in management, they appointed him the new Master of Ceremonies.

CHAPTER FOUR

A FEW REFORMS

THE domain to which Richard Nash now fell heir as King was a walled city of about twenty-five acres. Irregular sections of wall marked off this acreage from an amphitheatre of hills rising behind, while the river Avon, guarding Bath along its side opposite the walls, curved like two sickles laid handle against tip. Apart from the town-hall, in the market-place, the only building to impress a beholder from the hills on either side of the river was the Abbey Church, which reared its tall square tower above flanking tree-tops, but was hugged below by a litter of old houses in bad repair. Of the parts of Bath still lying vacant, not all were meadow or grove; here and there, the waters underneath seeped out in marshland.

The work confronting Nash, as he saw it with his managerial and legalistic eye, was to test his skill and patience for many a long year. Severely mindful of the recent tragedy, he began by abolishing the wearing of swords. He would 'hinder people from doing what they had no mind to'. Swords, he said, often tore the ladies' clothes, and frightened them by being drawn in their presence. But the law he framed was a piece of kingcraft more astute: 'None should ever wear a sword at Bath but such who were not entitled to wear it elsewhere'. So it was that the new Master of Ceremonies instituted democracy by a process of levelling up, whilst he regulated aristocracy by an edict that it levelled it down.

Having quietened the gaming-tables, he looked into

the room adjoining. The music of Webster's five local performers struck Nash as rustic. To urbanise it, he dismissed these musicians and engaged an orchestra of seven men from London, stipulating that they play also outdoors, by day, as at night in the town-hall. The extra cost he found by taxing each visitor a guinea as a 'music subscription', which provided for concerts both in the Grove and at the Cross Bath, the 'quality' bath. On the side of decorum, he did not like the custom of the sexes bathing together; but, one day at the Cross Bath, when a certain husband said his wife in the water 'looked so like an angel that he wished to join her', Nash, to confirm his own reputation as 'a man of gallantry and spirit', threw the husband in.

The Master inspected the lodging-houses, a procedure upon which Webster had never bestowed a thought. All of them were tawdry, and all rented at prices outrageously high. He found that gentlemen had to put up with rooms like garrets, unpainted, uncarpeted, grey with cobwebs, musty from stale air, even perilous: nails jutting from crossbeams menaced unwary heads. Householders described such rooms as 'elegant' if they contained coarse woollen hangings to stem the draughts, or if they boasted one or two creaky rush-bottom chairs more infirm than even the invalid guests. Nash gave terse orders that these coops be refitted, on pain of having them condemned, and for every room he fixed a tariff.

New decrees and improvements of such a nature were perhaps timely in a special sense, for Bath, just as Nash took over, was a bit frightened by a rumour. The formidable martinet, Dr John Radcliffe, physician to the royal family, said to have been 'affronted' by certain residents of Bath, retorted, so the story ran, that he would 'cast a toad' into the waters of its springs, and so draw away all the visitors to the rival spa of Tunbridge Wells. Whether Radcliffe had said so or not, the rumour evoked a scurrilous open letter to him from one Stopford, of Bath, who in August 1705 printed and circulated it. 'Great Sir', began

Stopford, 'We are informed by common fame, and certain evidence from your own mouth, when sober, that you are a professed enemy to our Bath-waters, that you vilify them as good for little or nothing'. From 'trifling pique and caprice', Radcliffe would 'put a toad in the waters, spoil the trade (in the waters, which Nash was already bottling officially and shipping round England), and bring lodgings down to half a crown a week'. The royal doctor was 'the great mountebank of the age', who 'loved claret so much that he would let his best friend die', and who had now 'wheedled some persons into leaving Bath for Tunbridge.' This 'railing out of pique' only showed Radcliffe's 'base birth and brutish temper'. Stopford posted a copy to the doctor, at Tunbridge.

In this outcry, Richard Nash undoubtedly noted all that was said about Tunbridge Wells. But, with his new London orchestra at his elbow, and thinking of the antidote of dancing after a tarantula's bite, he declared that he would fiddle the toad out of the waters, and stir every bather into such a dance that no venom could take effect. So airy a defiance won him the plaudits of the town.

At the moment he was more interested in a 'playroom', or theatre, at the top of Vicarage Lane, the first theatre to be opened in Bath. Funds wherewith to equip it came from subscriptions in the amount of £1,300, and the donors received recognition in the embellishment of the walls with their family arms. The 'room', with all seats at half a crown, held an audience of only 240, there was space for only one box, over the door, and the top row of seats reached to within four feet of the ceiling. The manager, scenery, costumes, music, playbills, and candles took two-thirds of the receipts, leaving £10 per night, if the house was full, to be divided between twelve actors. If this was but a meagre beginning, Nash could take some satisfaction in reflecting that before he ascended his throne Bath had no theatre at all.

Not content with a one-season Bath, the Master now announced two seasons, March until June, and October until Christmas. Amongst those who planned to come in March (1706) was the eminent elderly dramatist William Wycherley, the 'Plain Dealer', now sixty-five, long infirm from his rakish years, and now occupying himself mainly with writing verses for the scrutiny of a young friend, Alexander Pope. Wycherley was a patient of Dr Radcliffe. That the doctor nursed no resentment from the 'toad' episode is evident from a letter (22 March) from Wycherley to Pope: 'I have some thoughts of going from hence (Clive, near Shrewsbury) to the Bath, being advised to it by Dr Radcliffe when I was at London'.

While it is not certain that Wycherley made at this time his first sojourn in Bath, Nash would have welcomed him regally, though much preoccupied with finishing the Pump-room begun by Webster. On the site of three demolished houses along the south front of the Abbey, this new pavilion stood ready in the season of 1706 to open. No longer were the visitors to lack a semblance of a meeting-place outside the baths. For its opening, the Master drummed up a pageant in the style of the one he had staged for the late King in the Temple: a public procession, a musical fête, and a song (all to join in), composed especially for this day. In five six-line stanzas, the song exalted Bladud, the legendary invalid King cured at Bath. Nash, in the centre of the throng, as lawful successor to their ancient ruler, lost nothing by this representation.

The Pump-room was the property of the Corporation. But the Master promptly rented it from them, in order to make himself responsible for its operation. To regularise the dispensing of its waters, and so to fulfil the prescriptions of the resident doctors, he engaged an officer, whom he called the Pumper, and put him in charge. This man paid Nash for his post, making his money from tips. The straightening out of procedures at Bath was now gaining momentum.

Report of the new spirit animating the spot soon took

wing to town, and in the autumn the Master of Ceremonies was gratified by an influx of nobility. Robert Price, barrister of Lincoln's Inn, and judge, wrote of the scene in September to his friend Robert Harley, lately Secretary of State: 'The Bath has not been known at any time to be fuller than now it is, the Duke of Norfolk, the Duke of Beaufort, the Duchess of Shrewsbury . . . Lord Hyde, Lord Grantham, Lord Gore, Lord Granville . . . with abundance of ladies. The Duke of Norfolk is said to have a design upon Sir Nich. Sherburne's, of the North, daughter and heir, who is here also, who has upward of £3,000 per annum and red lettered. The Duke lives great both in table and equipage. Sir John Germaine . . . carried off £700 he won at play. . . . There are about fifty known gamesters and sharpers come here from London; they want cullies, and are forced to devour each other'.

Gamesters aside, such a congress of titled visitors imbued Nash with the determination to clean up and light the streets of Bath by law. The lighting, in winter, had been done hitherto by requiring householders to hang out lanterns. But the Corporation, on their own authority, had found it more difficult to compel the people to keep the public ways tidy. Nash persuaded the town in 1706 to apply to Parliament for special powers: to set a night-watch, to arrest vagrants, and to oblige the inhabitants to sweep the streets. One spot, the ancient town-market, held every Wednesday and Saturday, was an eyesore, left strewn with rubbish. So well-watered a town must needs wash its face, as now it began to do.

To attend to the streets within the walls was but to invite the question of the roads outside. Owing to ruts, rocks and ditches, a steep but picturesque climb, up Lansdowne Hill, was not only arduous for man but hazardous even for horses. In the same year another subscription—Nash was the guiding hand behind all such funds—amassed £1,800 to repair this road, 'that the invalids might conveniently ascend that hill, to take the benefit of the air upon it'. Ordinarily anyone who traversed these outer roads paid toll; visitors were now exempted from it on this route, the walk up Lansdowne being accounted a part of their cure.

Still Bath stood in need of a large general meeting-place for its guests. The Pump-room had its special function, at set hours; the shop for coffee was small, and privately run; and so was Horrid Tom's, popular in the sherry hour. For the rest, when the company wished to meet for tea or chocolate, they had to stand about in a booth. Nash discerned that if ever he was to get any cohesion in his 'subjects', and sustain a standard of style, dress, and deportment, he must provide a spacious room in which all could freely and comfortably assemble, take refreshment and play at cards. He had looked after their health; he would now do as much for their relaxation. In the spring of 1708, therefore, he engaged one Thomas Harrison to build an Assembly-House.

This hall, a single large room in the form of an oblong, and backed by the Terrace Walk, ran to about sixty feet in length, half that depth, and half that height, but with the upper third of its height in rafters supporting a peaked roof. On the long side facing away from Terrace Walk, Harrison added gardens with a double row of trees, extending right and left beyond the hall to the length of the hall itself. These gardens, 'for people of rank and fortune to walk in', he called Harrison's Walks. Like the Pumper, he had a financial 'arrangement' with Nash, to whom he paid three guineas a week for the privilege of managing the Assembly-House, but in turn made his own profit from the food and drink served.

The immediate effect of this new rendezvous was to transfer to it the dancing and the gambling from the town-hall, and unlike the town-hall, the Assembly-House was to be in operation both day and night. It yielded the Master fresh opportunity to levy 'subscriptions', which he promulgated to all visitors as a duty and an obligation, in default of which they were to leave Bath.

Nash now linked the charges of Pump-room and Assembly-House. Having at the request of the doctors moved his orchestra from the Grove to the Pump-room, he required the head of each family visiting Bath to pay two guineas for the music at the Pump and the balls at the Assembly, this fee entitling the family to three tickets for each ball—held on Tuesday and Friday nights. Nor were Harrison's Walks free. Those who took the air between dances, or who there promenaded by day, paid a guinea, a half-guinea, or a crown according to their means. The Master forbade all private parties or coteries, but invited everyone to the Assembly-House for concert-breakfasts, to dinner at three, and to tea at nine, an interval in the dancing. The ball began at six, and by order of the doctors mindful of the health of their patients, ended sharply at eleven.

Thus the regimen developed, ever more firmly under the hand of the autocrat. At the Pump-room, where to the sound of music the invalids drained at intervals three long-stemmed glasses, both morning and afternoon, there was a ladies' annex, to which the ladies paid a subscription to read newspapers and just to talk. At the bookseller's, they paid half a guinea or a crown to borrow books. At the coffee-house they paid a crown for pen and paper with which to write letters. No extra tax was demanded in cake-houses along the Avon, while lectures on art, like walks on the cliffs, appear to have been benevolently free.

Far from being rebelled against, all these rules and restrictions, payments and supplements, were accepted by the company at large. Within three years Richard Nash had made Bath the most fashionable watering-place in the country, and further, a place indeed that beckoned to continentals themselves, visitors to whom gambling was far less an attraction than the social milieu now emergent.

The Master drew up his Laws of Moses. The first decree in his decalogue he framed naturally for his own convenience: ladies of quality and fashion were not to expect—nor as ladies would they desire—visits of ceremony from the King of Bath at other times than upon their arrival and their going away. As for the gentlemen of fashion, any of them unaccustomed to appearing at levées of ladies in gowns and caps were to show breeding and respect. There was social rivalry in Bath: Nash ruled that no host 'take it ill' if any visitor went to the breakfast of another host. There was too much gossip in Bath for the good of the place: Nash exhorted his guests to regard the whisperers of scandal its authors.

But the thing upon which he most assiduously bent his discipline was deportment at the dances. To this aspect alone the Monarch devoted half of his code. No gentleman should give a ticket to a ball to anyone but a gentlewoman. Gentlemen who crowded in front of ladies at a ball showed bad manners. Since the question of precedence in dancing was troublesome, Nash forbade exhibitions of resentment from either gentlemen or ladies on the ground that someone had danced out of turn. Furthermore, children and elderly ladies showed a penchant at the Assembly for occupying the front seats, and thus impeding the dancers. Nash laid it down that such mere watchers be content with a second bench, inasmuch as they were either 'past or not come to perfection'.

Nash was no writer. He could not even write his own regulations in decent English; a pen in his hand 'numbed all his faculties'. Yet everyone who read these rules, posted up in the Pump-room, understood very well what the Master meant. The guests upon the whole were pleased, even eager, to obey, and in consequence Richard Nash himself rounded into a conspicuous personality, an individual character.

He dressed to fortify the part he was playing. No man in England had hitherto thought of wearing as a matter of habit a white hat. The King of Bath adopted a tricorne really cream-coloured, put it on well forward, until it grazed his right eyebrow, while to the left side of it he pinned a brooch. His wig was black; he knew the value of contrast. His ruddy face toned in with his brown coat, which was frogged, edged with lace, and thrust back as if to 'uncurtain' his inner costume ornate with more lace. At all seasons, regardless of the cold of winter, this Sultan of the Spa let his flowered waistcoat, like his coat, go unbuttoned, exposing his shirt bosom. It was as if he fancied 'a sweet disorder' in his dress. None dared gainsay his sartorial oddities, for any of which he had a ready reason if challenged. When a visitor asked why he always displayed his stock-buckle in front, Nash explained that he had a wen on his neck; it would pain him if pressed.

There was an old rake in London, Beau Feilding, who had bigamously married Barbara Villiers, the decrepit mistress of Charles II. The days of Beau Feilding, whether he was in or out of gaol, were numbered. The rising Beau, the man now to wear the title above all other contemporaries, a man given rather to making laws than to breaking them, was Richard Nash, and he was not marrying, bigamously nor otherwise.

CHAPTER FIVE

MEN OF LETTERS

BY the year 1709 the road between London and Bath had become a highway of national concern. Its 'exact measure' was taken 'by Mr. Tompion, clockmaker, in Fleet Street'. Stones were set up at every mile, 'to make travelling more agreeable'. The journey required two days and nights, and it was an adventure.

So ruggedly early in the morning did the coaches depart—from the Saracen's Head, in Friday-street near St. Paul's—that travellers slept at the inn on the night before. By supping together, they usually made some progress in acquaintance prior to setting out. If, as usual, there were more men passengers, they paid for the supper; otherwise the women paid. The travellers needed this meal. There was no breakfast for them until the coach pulled up at Colnbrook, twenty miles on, where the innkeeper, taking advantage of their besetting hunger made them 'pay very expensively'. Dinner at Reading was pleasanter; the host entertained them by 'waggery'. In such improved spirits did the company then resume the road that the order of the afternoon was 'songs and story-telling, with a bottle of Nantz passed round'. When they reached Theale they all alighted for cakes and ale. And nightfall put them down in Newbury, to devote the evening to 'carousing and tobacco', unless it were summertime, in which case gallantry engaged those equal to it, and 'pairing off'. Anyone bound for Bath except an invalid, it was assumed, was not averse to gaiety.

On the second day, another appallingly early start carried them as far as Marlborough for breakfast, their appetites whetted by the roads into that town, which were 'rocky, ridgy, and rutty'. It was then between Marlborough and Sandy Lane that the excitement had to be looked for, the 'light cavalry', or highwaymen. Anticipating a hold-up, the men in the coach hid their watches in their boots, and their guineas 'where the robbers always looked for them'. Nor, after such interruption, was the westward progress very comfortable in itself. On a long stretch of execrable road from Sandy Lane to Aquae Solis, if the coach did not get mired in a ditch or even overturn, it made at best two or three miles an hour. Travellers ruefully recollected the ease of their passage twenty-four hours earlier. But night, at last, brought the way-worn company into Bath, between whose six inns the driver distributed them.

Of these inns, although the White Lion, in the marketplace, was popular, the two most favoured by Beau Nash were the White Hart and the Bear, nearly opposite each other in Stall Street. The old White Hart, a landmark, was conspicuous for its gables, its commodious porch, and its leaded Elizabethan windows. Not so the Bear Inn, still older fashioned; from the street it displayed merely two curious antique red gates, with a wicket for visitors afoot; one passed the gates into a long stable-yard, and only then reached the inn. Invalids in chairs proceeded out of this yard to the baths. While Nash deferred to the 'carriage company' at both the Bear and the White Hart, upon whom he called on their arrival, and from whom he extracted their subscriptions, he often dined at the White Lion.

From some of the despoiled visitors he naturally heard of the highwaymen, and it did not leave the Beau unruffled that his guests should be robbed, except 'voluntarily' by gamesters in the Assembly-House of whom himself was one. To come empty-handed to Bath was not to contribute to its prosperity. While roads in good repair made the thieving of highwaymen more difficult, Nash could not endlessly raise subscriptions like the one for Lansdowne Hill. How much nearer Bath than Sandy Lane did these robbers think they could operate? It would be cheaper to drive them back than to repair more distant stretches of highway. Wherefore, whenever the Master heard of hold-up men creeping into the vicinity of Bath, he sent agents out to catch them. Robberies grew fewer. Within a comfortable radius the safety of his kingdom was assured. And at the same time Nash reduced the likelihood of disorder within the gates by getting Bath exempted from the quartering of soldiers.

Yet in respect of the gamblers whom he tolerated the Beau did not escape a satirical thrust. Ever since the spring of this year (1709), Dick Steele's periodical, the *Tatler*, had been acquiring national influence, and in August it printed a letter from Bath: 'The sharpers are now become so formidable here that they have divided themselves into nobles and commons. Beau Bogg, Beau Pert, Rake and Tallboy are of their upper house; broken captains, ignorant attorneys, and such other bankrupts from industrious professions, comprise their lower order . . . I cannot express to you with what indignation I behold the noble spirit of gentlemen degenerated to that of private cut-purses . . . all who care for their country or posterity, and see the pernicious effects of such a public vice, may endeavour its destruction by some effectual laws'.

Steele did not harp upon this one thing; but since his purpose was to satirize follies, he considered, two months later, another side of life at Bath that Nash had let run to excess. It had become the fashion, even the craze, of doctors in London and other large towns to close their offices during the season and flock to Bath. This strategy seemed to be an easy method of picking up new patients; but it rather curtailed the practice of the doctors who lived in Bath, and who were really more knowledgeable in the regimen of the waters. Since the final paragraph of a *Tatler* was usually pointed, if not barbed, Steele wound up his issue of 6 October with this injunction: 'Letters have been sent to Mr. Bickerstaff, relating to the present state of the town of Bath, wherein the people of that place have desired him to call home the physicians. All gentlemen therefore of that profession are hereby directed to return forthwith to their places of practice; and the stage-coaches are required to take them in before other passengers, till there shall be a certificate signed by the Mayor or Mr. Powell (a puppet-show man) that there are but two doctors to one patient left in town'.

Whether Nash discouraged these superfluous doctors or not, he made good use of the power of puppet-show men. Instead of prohibiting outright the wearing of boots in the Assembly-House—another step toward urbanising Bath away from Webster's bucolic license—the Beau produced a performance of puppets in which Punch, as a country squire booted and spurred, not only wore his boots all day but insisted on going to bed in them. Simultaneously Nash wrote and circulated a rhymed 'invitation to the Assembly' in which he ridiculed both men in boots and women in aprons:

> Come, Trollops and Slatterns,
> Cockt hats and white aprons,
> This best our modesty suits;
> For why should not we,
> In dress be as free,
> As Hogs-Norton squires in boots?

By degrees this devious attack yielded gratifying results. Fewer boots appeared on the floor, fewer aprons, and since the puppet Punch, in ranting about 'his town' had said that 'the ladies often moved minuets in riding-hoods', the riding-hoods as well began to disappear under Nash's process of 'civilising' the Assembly. The women had only to doff their excrescences of countrified attire, while the men, taking their cue from the 'London set', substituted pumps and silk stockings for boots. So it came about that the Master democratised his public

The King's Bath (filled from a hot spring at its centre), and at the left, the Pump-Room

The Minuet as danced, with restraint, in the Assembly-room

'What a large quantity of ground was hid under spreading petticoats, and what little patches of earth were covered by creatures with wigs and hats'.—Richard Steele, M.P.

entertainments, with the result that nobility no longer refused to mingle with gentry; all united with one another to heighten the refulgence of Bath. The Hierophant proclaimed that visitors had to do their duty, which was to attend; and attendance implied the authorised dress.

Nor was dress the only thing that mattered. Nash reached the conclusion that speech, word of mouth, equally needed overhauling. While it is difficult to say in which particulars, and how soon or how late, the *Tatler* swayed conduct at Bath, these papers were affecting the whole country. If the Beau did not fall in with Steele's views on gaming and doctors, he obviously did uphold him in the crusade against duelling. Again, in February 1710 Steele addressed not Bath especially, but his compatriots in general, on the nuisance of swearing, as it emanated from bores who were either 'phlegmatic' or 'choleric'. Not so much that swearing was profane, but that it proceeded from 'dulness and barrenness of thought', and those addicted to it were an infernal pest. With all this, Nash heartily agreed. He let it be known that swearing was out of order in the public rooms of Bath. The 'seasons' were lengthening at these waters. Summer and winter, the town was becoming the national resort. It must be known afar as a place that was neither dull nor coarse.

Nor was dancing, even as today in England, any laughing matter. Part of Nash's decorum, it seemed, was to preserve gravity or impassivity of countenance whilst taking pleasure with music, lest a cheerful face, not to mention a smile, betray lack of virtue, or of prudence, or of discretion. The features were out of tune with the instruments, as if the dancers were tone-deaf, and of course many of them were. If the ladies identified a straight face with modesty, fear of making a misstep seemed to govern the studious visages of the gentlemen. In the minuets, danced by one couple at a time, the lady being led to the centre of the floor by Beau Nash himself, this sedateness, observed by all, set the example for the country-dances which followed at the end of two hours. Ladies in ostrich-plumes and hoop-skirts, their partners in tricornes and silks, all were actually grateful to the Master for the solemnity of the dancing. They wanted their pomp not untrammelled, but measured by the yard. As a later novelist said, Nash, the one Philosophic Beau, held it axiomatic that the social English required tyrannical government as much as the political were able to dispense with it.

Indeed an observant visitor at this time found Nash thus enthroned. In 1711 an energetic pamphleteer aged fifty, Daniel Defoe, who in London was editing a second-rate periodical, the *Review* (which hardly competed with Addison and Steele), but who was also writing politically for Robert Harley the statesman, came through Bath gathering material for a book to be called *Tour Thro' Great Britain*. He was really eavesdropping for Harley. Defoe was a lean hawk-nosed man, innocent-eyed, but not accepted by the wits of St. James's as one of theirs because he turned either Whig or Tory with no more conscience than a weathercock. Now sizing up Richard Nash, Defoe later remarked: 'He is as one may say Director-General of the pleasures wherever he comes, is much caressed, and everyone seems to submit with delight, so much is he esteemed by the regulations he imposes with regard to decorum and the economy of the place'.

Harley, however, wanted to hear in particular Defoe's report on the local electorate, the people domiciled continuously in Bath: 'There is a very great narrowness of spirit in most of the inhabitants at Bath. They have but their seasons, and they are so hungry by that time they come about, that they look upon a newcomer as a person to be shared and divided amongst them . . . when they receive a favour at your hands, it is with such an air as if it were their due, and they quitted scores with you by their acceptance of it'. Robert Price, writing to Harley from Bath a few years before, had been too absorbed in dukes to notice this side, the information that Harley really sought.

'Everyone', Jonathan Swift in this same year of 1711 noted, 'is going to the Bath'. But by 'everyone' he did not mean Defoe, with whom he had no truck. Swift was thinking rather of men like his friend Joseph Addison, who he said 'had wit enough to give reputation to an age'. It was early in August that Addison handed over the *Spectator* to Steele for a month, and with Ambrose Phillips (Namby Pamby) drove down to the kingdom of Nash. Swift duly reported to Stella, 'Mr. Addison . . . is gone to Bath with pastoral Phillips for his eyes'. Addison at thirty-nine, writing most of the daily paper which was earning him renown as Sir Roger de Coverley, was wearing out a constitution never very sturdy. He was sallow, blue-eyed, weak of chin; but he held his head high, and from his finely modelled lips came a remarkable 'wit and nature heightened with humour'. Phillips, a minor 'beau' who wore red stockings and liked to hang his conversation up in the air, gave to Addison occasional verses for the paper, but pursued him in the hope of preferment as soon as the Whigs were returned. Such a notable man as Addison seldom went a journey unaccompanied.

There is no record of any passage of wit between Addison and Nash. But Addison, within a month after his visit, printed an account of a 'whistling match' at Bath, for a prize of a guinea, between a ploughman, an 'undercitizen', and a footman. Hundreds watched these men compete whilst a merry-andrew on the stage tried to grin them out of countenance. The footman outwhistled the others by mingling a Scotch tune with an Italian sonata, a hybrid too ghastly to laugh at. Addison said this account was sent him by a 'correspondent', out of regard to whom, and 'in regard to the public', he 'castrated' the recital of the performance.

It was a season of celebrities in Bath, although Lady Orkney, peevishly writing to Lady Oxford, said she found 'no conversation, nothing played at but dice', and Bath a town 'without one reasonable creature in it'. In October, Wycherley joined the scene, last column of the peristyle of 'confident young men' who once surrounded King Charles. Hearing that Henry Cromwell, a mutual friend of himself and Pope, was there, ill, the Plain Dealer went to see him. Cromwell was a Lincolnshire gentleman, original when not trying to be an author, who hunted foxes in the country and ladies in the town or in Bath.

Pope, after profiting much from his youthful association with old Wycherley, was now in course of 'dropping' him. The young poet had just triumphed with his *Essay on Criticism*, he was feeling independent, and at twenty-three he found rather time-consuming the intimacy of a man of seventy-one whose mind was beginning to give way. But Pope made as if to keep up appearances, while Wycherley was loath to believe he was no longer helpful. 'Mr. Wycherley', Cromwell advised Pope at the end of October, 'visited me at the Bath in my sickness, and expressed much affection to me; hearing from me how welcome his letters would be, he presently writ to you . . . I could not possibly be in the same house with Mr. Wycherley, tho' I sought it earnestly . . . but whenever we met we talked of you. He praises your poem, and even outvies me in kind expressions of you. As if he had not wrote two letters to you, he was for writing every post; I put him in mind he had already.' Cromwell had wanted to return to London with Wycherley, but found him 'engaged with others'. There were men of note in Nash's domain who still sought after the Plain Dealer. His hair had gone white; his eyes were reminiscent of pain; two creases from the inner ends of his eyebrows ran deeply up his forehead; but Wycherley in figure was godlike still, a man whose frame, when Nash should double his own years, the Beau of Bath might well envy.

Whilst Addison was in Bath, his partner Steele printed in the *Spectator* a letter, supposedly from one Simon

Honeycomb, revealing the ways and wiles of fortune-hunters at the waters. Fortune-hunting was now an established occupation in Bath, where those needy gentlemen of the chase found that they could meet endowed young ladies whose houses in town they could never have hoped to enter. After a season or two of practice at minor resorts like Epsom and Scarborough, young Honeycomb in the autumn made for Bath:

'I found a sober modest man was always looked upon by both sexes as a precise unfashioned fellow of no life or spirit. It was ordinary for a man who had been drunk in good company, or passed a night with a wench, to speak of it next day before women for whom he had the greatest respect. He was reproved, perhaps, with a blow of the fan, or an Oh, fie! But the angry lady still preserved an apparent approbation in her countenance. He was called a strange wicked fellow, a sad wretch; he shrugs his shoulders, swears, receives another blow, swears again he did not know he swore, and all was well. You might often see men game in the presence of women, and throw at once for more than they were worth, to recommend themselves as men of spirit. I found . . . that the loosest principles and the most abandoned behaviour carried all before them in pretensions to women of fortune . . .

'I was now in the twenty-seventh year of my age, and about the forty-seventh of my constitution, my health and estate wasting very fast, when I happened to fall into the company of a very pretty young lady in her own disposal . . . The young thing was wonderfully charmed with one that knew the world so well and talked so fine . . . and with a very little application the pretty thing has married me . . . I do now as much detest the course I have been in . . . as ever I did before I entered into it . . . I am weary of vice . . . it was not in my natural way . . . I am now so far recovered as not to bring this believing dear creature to contempt and poverty for her generosity to me . . . tell the youth of good education of our sex that they take too little care of improving themselves in little things; a good air at entering into a room, a proper audacity in expressing himself with gaiety and gracefulness, would make a young gentleman of virtue and sense capable of discountenancing the shallow impudent rogues that shine among the women'.

This confession of a reformed rake was perhaps plausible enough. Not every sporting young man in Bath who married a fortune was incorrigible. Under the vigilance of Nash, 'vice' was said to 'lose half its evil in losing all its grossness'. But he had a sharp eye for a desperado, against whom he took it upon himself to intervene with the family of the young lady whose future lay in jeopardy. By this time, the Master was taking the same line as protector of young men of means, if he found them growing too involved with adventuresses.

Whether Nash was nettled or not by the aspersions upon Bath for which Steele was responsible, the Master was able to say that Steele had published only hearsay, or concoctions. Not until 1713 did 'good Dick' venture to visit Bath in person. He had just been elected M.P. for Stockbridge, and he went down to the waters for a week to recuperate. Long done with the *Spectator*, and now bringing to an end its successor the *Guardian*, he decided to devote one of his two final papers to what he saw and experienced in Bath. He had heard that 'more constitutions were weakened there than repaired', and that 'the physicians were not more busy in destroying old bodies than the young fellows in producing new ones'. Jests of this kidney he had 'heard' before; he was now to see for himself, this brown tubby merry-eyed man, with an 'embroidered cap and brocade nightgown'.

One of Steele's first observations was a tribute to the work of Beau Nash: 'It was no little satisfaction to me to view the mixed mass of all ages and dignities upon a level, partaking of the same benefits of nature, and mingling in the same diversions'. He watched the dancers on their way to the minuets: 'I sometimes entertained myself by observing what a large quantity of ground was hid under spreading petticoats, and what little patches of earth were covered by creatures with wigs and hats'. He went to the baths, 'where the distinctions of sex and condition are concealed, and where the mixture of men and women hath given occasion to some persons of light imagination to compare the Bath to the fountain of Salmacis, which had the virtue of joining the two sexes into one person; or to the stream wherein Diana washed herself when she bestowed horns on Actaeon. But by one of a serious turn these healthful springs may rather be likened to the Stygian waters, which made the body invulnerable; or to the river of Lethe, one draught of which washed away all pain and anguish in a moment'.

In both *Tatler* and *Spectator* he had published letters touching upon 'scandal' at Bath. But during his week's visit Steele must have grown aware of the views of Beau Nash on that subject, views which held that scandal was 'the mark of a foolish head and a malicious heart', bringing more suspicion upon the propagator than upon the person abused. At all events the Captain, even in jest, now sought to cleanse reputations as the waters restored bodies. He defended gambling, on the ground that a man who lost with serenity was a philosopher, while one who stormed over it would have made a valuable soldier. The gravity of the players at Harrison's table reminded him of a council-board, and their concentration upon the cards dispelled the notion that gaming was an idle life. Thus to raise a fortune was to enlarge one's mind. Wealth, regardless of its source, won a man respect in the world.

It also gratified him to see the ladies at these games, acquiring 'such a boldness as raises them near that lordly creature man'. Here they learned contempt of wealth, and overcame their weakness of 'natural tenderness', sacrificing the fortune of their children like a Spartan or a Roman dame. To cast dice was the ideal way 'to display the well-turned arm, and to scatter to advantage the rays of the diamond'. Yet he was sure the gamester-ladies were above these vanities of showing their beauty, since they here distorted their faces, and 'wore their lilies and roses in tedious watching and restless lucubrations'. What they really craved was to emulate manhood: 'In spite of all slanders, their confidence in their virtue keeps them up all night, with the most dangerous creatures of our sex. It is to me an undoubted argument of their ease of conscience that they go directly from church to the gaming-table, and so highly reverence play as to make it a great point of their exercise on Sundays'.

The Abbey Church itself (which Steele did not write of) a singularly fine example of 'late Perpendicular', and called from its abundance of stained glass the 'Lantern of the West', had not always inspired the reverence it was designed to convey, for all its great west window of seven lights, framed with carved angels climbing and descending Jacob's ladder. The sides of some of the pews had had to be raised to stop the ogling during services between the sexes; there was a passing of notes from one pew to another, and 'the ladies were the only saints certain worshippers came there to adore'.

Steele concluded his paper with a few remarks upon the cure he took. Meeting with an embarrassment of physicians, he saw no reason to tone down what he had printed in the *Tatler* about their superfluity. He said he was cured in a week of more distempers than he ever had in his life. A learned fellow-lodger gave him 'a little something' to keep up his spirits; next day another enlivened him with 'an order to bleed' for his fever; a third proffered a specific for scurvy; and a fourth—probably noticing Dick's rotundity—wrote him a recipe for dropsy, free. When an apothecary, sent by a fifth well-wisher, pressed upon him a dose of physic, Steele remonstrated that he never took it, whereat the man guessed that this patient was a doctor himself. Such 'oppression of civilities' frightened the new M.P. out of enquiring what the actual baths would do to him. However, he urged that every man who had benefited from Bath ought within the limit of his purse to improve, adorn, or recommend it'. 'A Prince should found hospitals; the noble and the rich may diffuse their ample charities. Mr. Tompion gave a clock to the Bath, and I, Nestor Ironside, have dedicated a *Guardian*'.

This was the most extensive notice, in writing, given to Bath by a distinguished author since the arrival of Nash eight years before. The satire in it might prove a slow corrective; but the humour of it was so engaging that the remedial hints it contained might well begin to bear fruit before long. It is not known how far Steele impelled the Master of Ceremonies to take action: but Nash did do away with the apparent impropriety of men and women going into the same bath at the same time.

In the following summer, Queen Anne having died on 1 August, and the Duke and Duchess of Marlborough on the same day having landed in England after two years of political exile in Flanders, the Marlboroughs, tarrying in London only ten days for a round of welcome, made their appearance in Bath. Nash gave them a sonorous greeting of eight bells. The Duke, though sixty-four, was the stalwart hero still, with fire in his dark eye and the air of command not put off. If, as Swift said, he was 'ambitious as hell and covetous as the prince of it', nobody any longer feared his ambition. Duchess Sarah was ten years younger, and looked it; pugnacious, calculating, dashing, she was not the blonde beauty of her roseate days; yet she retained her old assertiveness, and she was eager to resume a dominant place in the life of England, a great lady if no longer a power in statecraft. Always with an eye for character in others, she looked upon Beau Nash, now only forty, and although she and the Duke stayed in Bath but two or three days, the Duchess found the Master of Ceremonies a most engaging man.

The soldier whose work was done was followed in September to Bath by the poet whose work was beginning. Alexander Pope had now capped his remarkable *Essay on Criticism* with *The Rape of the Lock*, a feat even more celebrated, and at twenty-six, his genius acknowledged, he was foremost of English poets. This son of a linen-draper was a misshapen little man only four and a half feet tall, with a nose too large for his face, a leathery skin, and eyes shining like planets. For half of his young lifetime he had been hobnobbing with men-of-letters, until latterly, indeed, he was teaching some of these grandfathers how to suck eggs. Almost everything was to be forgiven a poet of genius. Pope was asserting the triumph of mind over the distortion of body. But those to whom poetry was not the highest achievement of living man were perhaps finding it difficult to excuse this grotesque little visitor's arrogance, his self-esteem, his impudence. These qualities Pope was quick to detect but slow to smile at in others; to him, the strut and flourish of Beau Nash were impudence personified.

It was very like Pope to pin his own foibles upon someone else. Old Wycherley was again in Bath; benefactor and benefited could not avoid occasional meetings, and from time to time the company in the public rooms saw them standing together, the venerable dramatist towering a foot and a half above his stunted but famous friend. Pope, who did not often smile, was possibly unaware that the dominant sense of humour in Wycherley, senile though he now was, led him to play iconoclast, to mock at the gravity of one like Pope when it became too ponderous. At the end of September, Pope wrote to his neighbour John Caryll, at Binfield, who was also Wycherley's friend: 'I walk about here as innocently, and as little dreaded, as that old Lion in Satire, Mr. Wycherley, who now goes tame about this town ... He that dares to despise the great ones of this age, to deny common sense to Ministers of State, their small portion of wit to the poets, and honesty to maids of fourteen ...'

But Pope was having a good time, and he did not let the 'old lion in satire' occupy too much of it. His semi-sentimental friends, the Blount sisters, were seldom out of his mind, and to the handsomer one, the blonde

Martha, he sent word about ten days later (6 October) of his adventures: 'If I may ever be allowed to tell you the thoughts I have so often of you in your absence it is at this time, when I neglect the company of a great number of ladies to write this letter. From the window where I am seated I command the prospect of twenty or thirty in one of the finest promenades in the world, every moment that I take my eye off from the paper. If variety of diversions and new objects be capable of driving our friends out of our minds, I have the best excuse imaginable for forgetting you, for I have slid I cannot tell how into all the amusements of the place; my whole day is shared by the pump-assemblies, the walks, the chocolate-houses, raffling-shops, plays, medleys, etc. I endeavour (like all awkward fellows) to become agreeable by imitation, and observing who are most in favour with the fair, I sometimes copy the civil air of Gascoin' (Richard Gascoigne, a troublesome Jacobite) 'sometimes the impudent one of Nash, and sometimes, for vanity, the silly one of a neighbour of yours, who has lost to the gamesters here that money, of which the ladies only deserve to rob a man of his age'.

On the walks he saw something of his friend Thomas Parnell, the Irish poet and divine. But Pope again playfully informed the Blount sisters that he had grown 'so dissipated and perverse', and was 'so much a rake', that he was 'ashamed of being seen with Dr. Parnell. I ask people abroad "who that parson is?" '

Like George Berkeley, that other learned vicar from Dublin, Parnell fraternised with the poets of London. He was a friend of young John Gay, so endearing a character round town that not even Pope was able to be unkind to him. Gay had written the poem *Wine*, to deny that water-drinkers could ever succeed as authors; and he had then attracted still more attention with *The Present State of Wit*. He was a frolicsome fellow: a broadside of the day ran: 'See Johnny Gay on porter's shoulders rise'. Titled ladies employed him as 'secretary' for the sake of being entertained by his sparkling humour. But it was Gay's dedication of *Rural Sports*, a biographical poem, to Pope, in 1713, that put him on a firm footing of affection with that poet, and it was no doubt through Pope that Gay and Parnell met. From both Parnell and Pope he now heard a good deal about Bath, with the result that in the spring following Pope's visit to the waters (March 1715) Gay wrote to Parnell of a plan to meet them both there, if all could so arrange their summer plans.

'You shall preach', Gay proposed to Parnell, 'and we will write lampoons, for it is esteemed as great an honour to leave the Bath for fear of a broken head, as it is for a Terrae Filius of Oxford to be expelled'.

With the addition of John Gay in prospect, Beau Nash could fairly consider that the literary pace of Bath had been set. He could now reasonably expect that the patrons of poetry, whose presence likewise would enhance the attraction of the resort, would follow their favourite authors to the Assembly-rooms. The new reign of George I was safely carrying on the fashion begun in the last years of Anne.

CHAPTER SIX

A POSTAL-CLERK

HAVING established Bath as the most fashionable spa in England, Nash was anxious to maintain its primacy. Amongst the local people he was aware of a certain measure of jealousy of Tunbridge Wells, a jealousy not diminished by the identity of Dr Radcliffe with Tunbridge in recent years. But Radcliffe was now dead, dead of gout at sixty-four; the way was clear for Nash to take a look at the other waters himself. He presumably reckoned that if Tunbridge was to thrive, it should do so not under the direction of a rival Beau, but governed from Bath, and thus be kept in its proper relation to his major resort.

There was in fact cause for some concern. The advantage of Tunbridge over Bath lay in its accessibility: only 36 miles from London, a drive of a mere four or five hours. Its chalybeate waters were 'pleasingly steely', at their best from May until October, and while the Wells offered no hot baths, it did provide a refreshingly cool one, which was all that summer visitors required.

Nestled between two Sussex hills, Mt. Sion and Mt. Ephraim, Tunbridge was the gathering-place of invalids almost wholly, rather than of pleasure-seekers. Its amusements were 'neither elegant nor diverting'; in consequence the company remained disunited and unsocial. 'The daily life of Tunbridge', it was said in 1714, 'hath no other variety but new faces, and those we have, beautiful, every day. The Sussex fresh-coloured lasses, in their high-crowned hats, are no small ornament to the place. I believe there is no place in the world better to begin an intrigue in than this, nor than London to finish it'.

Facility of 'intrigue' resulted from the circumstance that Tunbridge practised no more ceremony than Montpellier—the resort of the English in Restoration days. 'You engage with the ladies at play without any introduction, only they do not admit of visitors at their lodgings; but every gentleman is equally received by the fair sex upon the walks. The sharpers are the first that bid you beware of sharpers when they design themselves to pick your pockets. All shopkeepers are in fee with these fellows, and furnish them with dice'.

The daily programme was simple enough. Visitors drank the waters early, then dressed, and congregated in the coffee-houses. After hearing the news and gossip, they promenaded on the Pantiles, where musicians played. Tea was there served until two o'clock—dinner-time. Bowling-greens occupied the company through the afternoon. In the evening they resumed their walks along the Pantiles, or (four times a week) went to a ball, or gambled until midnight. While a considerable part of this daily round resembled the customs at Bath, it was ill-regulated, and lacked appeal to visitors of rank not prepared to dispense with their prerogatives. In the crudity of the arrangements at Tunbridge lay the opportunity of the Master of Ceremonies from Bath. Nash had only to instil, with variations, the discipline he had already found fruitful, in order not only to refashion Tunbridge but to make it add to his own welfare. He must investigate.

As at Bath, these changes should come by degrees. The Beau had in Bath far too much to supervise to allow him to spare for Tunbridge more than fleeting visits. In this year 1715, nearly 8,000 visitors made holiday in Bath. And they had their excitement. A young postal-clerk, Ralph Allen, discovered that a shipment of arms was being sent from the west into Bath to outfit a band of Jacobites who were to march in support of the larger forces of rebels in the North. No one suspected Allen of opening letters; yet he was an agent of the Government, and he did have unusual sources of information. He proceeded to inform General George Wade, who was the ranking officer then in Bath. Wade acted promptly, Bath continued serene, and the General in gratitude took young Allen under his wing.

At first sight there was nothing prepossessing about this postal-clerk. Under a capacious forehead his eyes were small but shrewd, his mouth a straight line, and his nose something fox-like. Aged only twenty-one, he was thin and solemn-looking, with long fingers and thin legs. He was the son of an innkeeper in Cornwall; but Allen as a boy spent less time at the inn than at the local post-office, where his grandmother was in charge. In this post-office a passing inspector noticed him, and got for him, at eighteen, a vacancy in the post-office at Bath. And now another vacancy arose: the postmastership itself. Through the influence of General Wade, Allen was appointed.

During these early years of Allen in Bath it is unlikely that he had any personal acquaintance with the Master of Ceremonies. As postmaster, however, Allen became a dignitary whom it was convenient for Nash to know. At all events, in 1716, the question of a hospital for the poor was first discussed by both residents and visitors, and in the plans for such a long-needed amenity Allen as well as Nash showed uncommon interest. As Steele had said in the *Guardian*, 'a Prince should found hospitals' in Bath. It was a coincidence that a Princess of Charity, Lady Elizabeth Hastings, whom Steele in his *Tatler* had immortalised by the line 'to love her was a liberal education', now proposed the founding in Bath of a general hospital for the benefit of 'poor diseased objects'. The words of this beautiful young widow—this sort of plain-clothes nun, who in order to keep control of her fortune refused to remarry, and was devoting her life to study, religion, and helping the poor—her words carried weight, like her philanthropic purse. So extensive, however, was the design which enthusiasts for the hospital had in mind, so large was the sum required to set the scheme going, and so difficult was the purchase of land at once desirable and reasonable, that progress was for an indefinite period bound to be slow.

Unfortunately for the immediate prospects of the hospital, visitors who were charitably inclined sometimes chose to devote their funds to improvements less needed. In this same year one Humphrey Thayer, described as 'a wealthy druggist' of London, bought two plots of land, the old bowling-green and the orchard of the Abbey, with a view to adorning the sites by building upon both. While this outside interest was encouraging to Nash, it hardly helped him in his new determination to extend the benefits of Bath to the moneyless infirm.

To this end, he was cheered by the return to Bath in August of the Marlboroughs, although the Duke had suffered a stroke, and had come specifically to mend what he called his 'palsy'. Within a week or two he convalesced to a surprising degree. Word of it got round, and on 20 August Lady Cooper wrote from Hampton Court to the Duchess: 'It is with the greatest delight imaginable that I hear from everybody that the Duke of Marlborough is so much recovered by the Bath. His life and health is a public good, and wished for by everybody . . . I fancy you've got the Duchess of Shrewsbury at the Bath by this time'.

If the response of the Duchess of Marlborough (3 September) would have raised only mixed feelings in Nash, it gave the amenities of Bath their due: 'Her Grace of Shrewsbury is here, and of a much happier temper. She plays at ombre upon the walks, that she may be sure to have company enough, and is as well pleased in a great crowd of strangers as the common people are with a bull-baiting or a mountebank'. This mingling of the classes was of course one of Nash's set aims. 'I have been upon the walks but twice, and I never saw any place

Queen Square. Built in 1728 by John Wood (1705–54), associate of Beau Nash in the development of Bath

Beau Nash's House, St. John's Court. Built in 1720 by Thomas Greenway, it was bought and occupied by Nash when he was aged 46

abroad that had more stinks and dirt in it than Bath, with this difference only, that we are not starved, for here is great plenty of meat, and very good, and as to the noise, that keeps one almost always awake. I can bear it with patience, and all other misfortunes, as long as I think the waters do the Duke of Marlborough any good'.

The Duke had been feeling well enough to play at piquet with Dean David Jones, at sixpence a game. One night the Duke, when winner one game, left off, and asked for his sixpence. Jones had no silver. Later the Duke renewed his demand, and when the Dean repeated his excuse, Marlborough insisted that he change a guinea, since the Duke wished to pay for a chair to carry him home. Jones got the change, and complied. Soon afterward he saw the Duke leave the Assembly-room and walk home, to save the sixpence which the chair would have cost him.

His relatively reckless Duchess, on the contrary, played high, and resented any interruption at the tables for such purposes as a walk to the bookseller's. 'Books!' she exclaimed. 'Prithee don't talk to me about books! The only books I know are men and cards'. Clearly if the Governor of Bath, as Nash during this season was being called, was to interest the Marlboroughs in the projected hospital, a cause not alien to reducing the 'stinks and dirt' of Bath, it was to the Duchess alone, and not to the thrifty Duke as well, that he must introduce a subject so costly.

Upon such personages as the Duchess, whom he pleased, Nash needed not fear that sooner or later he should fail to exert his influence. Yet he had his detractors, his traducers, wretches who either from envy or out of revenge for some reversal of fortune which they laid at his door sought to unking him. In the year following, 1717, an anonymous writer published a booklet called *Court Tales*, in which he abused Nash under the name 'Nessus', but obligingly explained in the back of the book that the name stood for 'N-s-h'. The tribute ran:

'Nessus, a common sharper, who to the scandal of the

quality of the island, was admitted into their cabinets when he ought to have been sent to the gibbet. The fellow was an odd composition of cowardice and impudence, of pleasantry and nonsense; and had he not been too much a rascal would have made a finished coxcomb. But a rogue has something too horrible in him to make a subject for satyr, and instead of making a jest of Nessus, one cannot think of him without trembling. So many bubbles has he reduced to beggary, so many heirs sent to the Armies, so many heiresses to the stews, yet in all public places who but Nessus for their pleasures? Nessus is treasurer to the ball, and banker to the basset. Nessus raps at my lady's bedchamber, and enters it as freely as if he was to dress her. Nessus calls for chocolate, and cries damn him, if it is not ready, for he has fifty visits to pay, and the ladies will be all stirring else. Nessus kisses the wife and cocks at the husband, lives with the women as Horner did' (the pseudo-eunuch in Wycherley's *Country Wife*) 'a seducer by profession, who lulls the vigilance of husbands by a cynical stratagem, and makes them introduce him themselves to their wives, and encourage his intimacy with them, because the husbands are in the hopes that he'll be contented with cheating them. He had the reputation of courage till he was kicked out of a coffee-house for want of half a crown to pay an old debt, and denying it rather than discover his indigence. For with all his bubbles, Nessus is himself a bubble, and spends on a common strumpet what the less common ones lavish on him'. The writer then accused him of relieving one 'Maura' of 400 crowns at the gaming-table, which sum the lady could not wholly pay, whereat Nessus 'had the gallantry to take her necklace in pawn for it, and at the next Assembly his own dirty mistress appeared with it, to the terrible mortification of Maura and the wonderful delight of the whole company'.

While these charges carried all the exaggeration of gossip, of scandal, the few grains of fact in them may well have led ingenuous people to believe more. Actually, if players at the tables were amateurs, unsuspecting women, or young persons, especially bridegrooms, Nash rather kept them from gambling away their assets than let them lose. By his own skill at games, he often won back little fortunes which the unwary lost to the professionals, and restored the money to the 'innocents', whom he then excluded from returning to the cards. Nash's tactics were sometimes brusque; he did not hesitate to snatch a dice-box from the hand of a visitor coasting to perdition. If now the Master of Ceremonies took any notice at all of *Court Tales* in respect of gambling, its charges could only cause him to intensify his vigil in the Assembly-room.

With regard to women, the case was somewhat otherwise, as one's private life may differ from one's conduct in public. It has been said that Nash did not long continue the 'universal gallant', as he had done toward the end of his stay in London. If during his first years in Bath, the years of establishing himself, the Governor gave up his endeavours to 'deceive the sex', in order to become the protector of the innocent, he did not altogether keep aloof from women who had been already 'deceived'. Now in his middle years, he was no ascetic. Nor yet was he in search of a wife; as a bachelor, he could better sustain his eminence, his command, and his popularity amongst both men and women visitors. Unlike Ralph Allen, who in 1720 sagaciously accepted in marriage the illicit daughter of his patron General Wade, Nash shied away from wedlock, although if he had surrendered, he was no man to take a bride from the left side of the blanket. His mistress was Fanny Murray, the comely daughter of a local musician. Before she lived with Nash she had been mistress to the Hon. 'Jack' Spencer.

One day Nash was told that a certain man in the coffee-room had called him a whoremonger. The Master sought out this man, of whom he demanded an explanation.

'I've been informed', said his accuser, 'that it is true'. 'Then you've been misinformed', retorted Nash. 'I acknowledge I have a woman living in my house. But if I do keep her, a man can no more be termed whoremonger for having one whore in his house than a cheesemonger for having one cheese'.

Of such was Nash's defence, if he thought it worth while to make any, against the allegations in *Court Tales* that he was as promiscuous as Wycherley's Horner.

The house in which the Beau and Fanny made themselves comfortable was a new house in St. John's Court, at the corner of Saw Close. This was 'the richest sample of building till then executed' in Bath, with three floors, five windows across the front, and six down the side, the roof being set off by a coping. The ground-floor windows and those of the storey above were very tall; each was ornamented at its top with a ledge. First of several houses built round this Court by one Thomas Greenway, a stone-cutter, apparently as a speculation, it was in proportions and in outward pretentiousness a 'mansion'. Indoors, not to disappoint, Greenway decorated its rooms in gilt and crystal. Nash chanced to look in. He thought the house fit for the King that he was, whereupon he bought it outright from Greenway. The front door of such a house must betoken the eminence of its tenant: Nash proceeded to flank the door with a pair of pillars on pedestals, which he crowned with a pair of great setting birds, long-billed, like cranes. 'Richest sample' of building in Bath that it was, this house at once began to draw the sightseers.

Amongst them appears to have been a certain attractive Mrs Lindsey, lately (1719) celebrated as one of the 'three nymphs' of that rival resort, Tunbridge Wells. The doggerel to Lindsey ran thus:

> As tawny Egypt once could boast
> A Queen so heavenly fair,
> Tho' she the earth's wide empire cost
> Was yet not thought too dear.

> So tempting Flavia is the pride
>   Of swarthy Tagus' shore,
> For her I'd Antony outbid,
>   And give a planet more.
>
> In naked charms her soul appears
>   Undrest of all disguise;
> Her freedom tempts, her wit endears;
>   Heaven opens in her eyes.

These quatrains inspired an 'Answer to the Three Nymphs':

> Fair Flavia without wandering far
>   As tawny Egypt's coast,
> With British beauties may compare,
>   Yet reign the favourite toast.

And this avalanche, signed 'The Satyrist', in turn provoked an 'Answer';

> On Lynsey's charms so I'll revere
>   As to say nothing of them here,
> But that she's witty and sincere.

It so happened that Nash, coincident with establishing himself in his new house, arranged with Harrison, his manager at the Assembly-rooms, to add to the Assembly a large ballroom. Harrison employed a designer of the name of William Killigrew to build a room thirty by sixty feet, separated from the original room by a staircase, and to be used primarily for the dances on the Tuesday evenings. Into this new room, in due course, swept Dame Lindsey, as a kind of hostess. She was described in Bath as 'a person who sang in the opera'.

The expansion of the Assembly-rooms to accommodate the swelling influx of visitors marked the beginning of the expansion of Bath itself. Prior to 1720, the dimensions of the town had been the same as those drawn by the Romans. Marshes were now filled in and staked for new roads, pastures levelled off and prepared for new houses. Killigrew, at the same time he was working on the new Assembly-room, broke ground for Weymouth House, which was to be the local retreat of the Thynne family.

Titled personages were no longer content with rooms or lodgings in Bath; they must have houses, owned if not rented.

Keeping pace with these new developments the Master of Ceremonies developed his 'home life' to scale. In St. John's Court the latch-string was out. Any friend who wanted a meal (at 2 p.m.) could have it. 'Come gentlemen!' said the Beau, 'eat and welcome; spare, and the devil choke you'. He provided plain dishes: boiled chicken or roast mutton. Small potatoes, which he called 'English pineapples', he took at the end of dinner, like fruit. His drink was small beer, with or without a glass of wine in it; or else wine and water. After the meal, he took one glass of wine. The evening meal, at nine or ten o'clock, was a hot supper, usually of breast of mutton and his potatoes. Soon after supper, unless he looked in at the gambling, he went to bed, not because he was an invalid like so many of the visitors, but because he wanted to keep from becoming one.

Thus he was able to get up early of a morning, at five o'clock. But this rather monastic rising the Master did not require of his servants; in consideration of them, whose rest he was careful not to disturb, he had his fire laid at the time he went to bed. In the morning he lit it himself, and sat by it to read, before going out. There was, a little later, a levée of sorts. Was he not a king? Buffoons, parasites, even his 'poet-laureate' came in, and read to him jingles of Bath—if asked.

Nash then sauntered out in his embroidered coat, which he called his 'advertisement'. 'That's the only use', said he, 'of a fine coat'. In white stock and beaver, ruffles and lace, he walked to the Pump-room and drank the waters, setting the example of regularity. He took a turn in Harrison's parade. Thence he proceeded to the coffee-house for breakfast. During the rest of the morning, until dinner-time, the Beau was an extremely busy man about town: he 'arbitrated differences' either amongst his neighbours or between the visitors; he ordered procedures with regard to the recreations of the day; he waited upon the new arrivals, at their lodgings or their houses, to pay his respects; and if he then had any time left, he received friends in St. John's Court. Not impervious to obeisance, whatever its source, if a beggar accosted him with 'Your Honour', Nash bowed; if the man said 'Your lordship', Nash gave him whatever money he had on him at the moment.

The Master of Ceremonies had by this time worked out his 'philosophy'; that healing ensued from change of scene, of climate, and of society, but that relaxation, to be of benefit, must be disciplined.

CHAPTER SEVEN

NOBLE VISITORS

WITHOUT ever travelling to foreign watering places himself, Nash was providing at home for the English the attractions they had hitherto found only abroad. It was said of his compatriots that they had visited Continental spas 'to the injury of their fortunes, their morals, and their patriotism'. In Bath, as one might say, they at least did no harm to their patriotism. The actual waters were probably as effective at one spa as at another; what Bath had lacked until the Beau refurbished it was 'social indulgence'. Once the English were assured of that, they were willing enough to change the scene of their outings.

Early in 1721 a rhymester, such as Nash's 'poet-laureate', presented the spectacle in these verses which he called 'The Pleasures of the Bath':

> The spring's a-coming,
> And Nature's blooming;
> Each amorous lover
> Does vigour recover;
> The birds are singing
> And flowers are springing;
> Here's toys to be raffled for,
> Who makes one?

> Best, past comparisons,
> At Mr Harrisons
> Dice are rattling,
> Beaux are prattling,
> Ladies walking
> And wittily talking;
> Madam, the Medley's just begun.

> Here's half a guinea
> To hear Nicolini;
> Pray give me a ticket:
> Main's seven, I nickt it.
> I'm going to Lindsey's;
> Spadilla wins ye;
> I'm baffled, by Jerrico,
> Quite undone!
>
> Bells are jangling,
> Chairmen wrangling,
> Cudgelling, thumping;
> Bathing and jumping,
> The way of the morning
> Is dressing, adorning,
> And then to the green,
> Where the ladies run.

And when spring had passed and summer was well along, auspiciously enough under these conditions, Nash in August was in Tunbridge, just to lend to its season the proper 'tone'. In his absence arrived at Bath the Countess of Bristol, for a 'hysterical disorder'. She found the place rather colourless without its leader. 'I have been', she wrote to her husband on 16 August, 'but three times at Lindsey's since I came, and once to Harrison's. Nash is not yet arrived, but is to come today.' Sad to say, the Beau dallied elsewhere, and three days later Lady Bristol resumed: 'The plays begin tonight, and I suppose all diversions will go forward now Governor Nash is arriving'.

By the end of the month Nash had indeed returned, to find in Lady Bristol, who was now forty-one, a face without curves, neither oval nor oblong, but big, an expanse, a façade, with cheeks full, forehead both high and full, and eyes rather masculine than feminine. There was no distinction in her features. The Master of Ceremonies confided to her that 'several gamesters were coming this week', and Lady Bristol, having been spoken to, no doubt felt an improvement in her hysterical disorder.

She was a friend of Peggy Bradshaw, another visitor, a lady described as 'a person of more gaiety than delicacy'.

Like many ladies, whether at Bath or in town, she set her cap at the poet of the season, jolly John Gay, who had left off going to Aix for Bath, whose *Poems*, lately published, were being read the country over, and upon whom it was now incumbent, when he was not immersed in the cure, to give a good deal of his attention to the lively Duchess of Shrewsbury, since she was his patroness. To Henrietta Howard, Countess of Suffolk, Mrs Bradshaw wrote on 30 August:

'I would fain persuade Mr Gay to draw his pen; but he is a lost thing, and the colic has reduced him to pass a humdrum hour with me very often. I desired him to club a little wit towards diverting you; but he said it was not in him; so I chose rather to expose myself, than not put you in mind of a poor sick body that has taken physic today and not seen the face of a mortal.'

If Peggy Bradshaw rather fancied flirtation than cards, the reverse was the case with the Countess of Bristol. The 'deep gamesters' were slow in turning up, and Lady Bristol began to revert to her hysterical disorders from worry over her absent husband. 'Mr Nash said', she wrote the Earl on 9 September, 'my countenance informed him more of your being near at hand than all the bells could do'. But when another ten days had rolled by, and no Earl, the behaviour of Lady Bristol impelled her friend Peggy to report to Henrietta Howard: 'The Countess finds her recreations; she cries every post-day for an hour because the Earl has not come; she dries up her tears about twelve, to play upon the walks, and an hour sooner, if anybody gives a breakfast (which happens about three times a week), we quarrel and are friends, and at it again after it is scolded out'.

Mrs Bradshaw thought Bath 'all noise and nonsense'. She did not fail to notice much of the 'nonsense'. William Congreve had just joined the visitors. Gouty at fifty and losing his eyesight, his face grown pudgy from soft living on Government sinecures, he was still the foremost comic dramatist of the age, still a man to contest with John Gay poetical primacy in Bath. Congreve was intimate with Henrietta, eldest daughter of the dying Duke of Marlborough, and heiress, as Duchess, to his title. But in Bath he was dallying with a Mrs Berenger, as the ubiquitous Peggy Bradshaw well noted. 'Mrs Berenger', she continued in the same letter, 'passes most of her time with Mr Congreve, who is in the house with her'.

Day by day, Peggy knew 'who was with whom'. 'I met Mr Gay by chance . . .' she went on, 'he is always with the Duchess of Queensberry, for we are too many for him; but that is only in your ear, for we have now and then a private conference at the pump'. It would not do for the Duchess to know that 'Johnny and Peggy' met, apart. 'I believe I shall go home dumb, for I make very little use of my talking faculty, for fear of a quarrel (with the capricious Lady Bristol). Nash says if I go off without one, my statue shall be set up in the town'.

The Beau risked many a quarrel himself, but was very seldom worsted from taking the chance. It was the Duchess of Queensberry who furnished one test of his authority. She was now twenty, and had been married to the Duke a little over a year. Though called as a maiden Lady Kitty Hyde, second daughter of the Earl of Clarendon, she was supposed to be a daughter of Lord Carleton. 'Whoever remembers Lord Carleton's eyes', said Lady Mary Wortley Montague later, 'must confess they now shine in the Duchess's face'. Carleton left her £5,000, also property in Wiltshire and Oxfordshire. Kitty, warm-hearted and eccentric, had thick wavy blonde hair, and languid plucked eyebrows; she was rather heavy-eyed; her Cupid's bow was her best feature. In order to rival her sister Jane, she had wished to 'go out into the world'. Her method of going out was to appear at Drury Lane. Matthew Prior, released from gaol in 1717 as a political prisoner, managed to get into Drury Lane on the night of Kitty's début, and so captivated was he by her winsomeness that he wrote to her a poem, 'The Female Phaeton' (published in 1719), in which he celebrated both Kitty's liberation from her family and her impression upon the audience. This poem ended:

> Tenderness prevail'd, Mama gave way;
> Kitty at heart's desire
> Obtained the chariot for a day,
> And set the world on fire.

With a pretty wit of her own, Kitty became a friend of the wits. She had her portrait painted as a milkmaid. Mrs Delany afterward said of this sprightly creature, 'Her wit, beauty, and oddities made her, from her early years, when she was (as Prior said) "Kitty beautiful and young", the general object of animadversion, censure, and admiration'.

And now she was in Bath a Duchess, the bride of a year, and for almost as long the patroness of John Gay. Having posed elsewhere as a milkmaid, the Duchess saw fit to give way to her eccentricity in Bath by appearing at the Assembly-rooms in an apron. She was perhaps unaware that the Master of Ceremonies had forbidden aprons to the ladies as he had abolished boots on men. True, the white apron worn by the young Duchess this night was of finest lace, and worth £200. But Nash magisterially came up to her, tore the apron off, and threw it away.

'Such things', said he with great aplomb, 'are suitable only for Abigails'.

The Duchess was too good-natured to resent this cavalier treatment. Instead of growing angry, she had humour enough to accept the censure as part of the evening's entertainment, of which the upshot was that she went so far, on the spot, as to 'beg his Majesty's pardon'.

But the triumphs of Nash at the dance were sometimes punctured by his defeats at the table. Still in September, even as he had been keeping a watchful eye upon the luck of other players, Lady Bristol wrote of him to her lord: 'I threw 15 mains yesterday morning, and got but £50 by it; Mr Nash said he had a great mind to write you a word of it. Mr Nash lost £50 a Saturday at

Harrison's and as they say broke all the windows according to custom'.

Lady Bristol, for her part, endeavoured by medicinal aid to keep down her 'hysterical disorders' sufficiently to enable her to gamble with care, although she was of two minds about her doctor. 'The sight of Dr Cheyne this morning', she informed the Earl, 'renewed my affliction; but he has given me something that has done me a vast deal of good'.

The worthy Dr George Cheyne, also Nash's doctor, carried almost the dimensions of a hippopotamus. He was now fifty. At thirty, in London, he had become a *bon viveur*, in order to get patients. This expanding habit of life had put so much fat on him that he had in recent years come to Bath to live on milk and vegetables, intending, as soon as he had lost a few stone, to give part of his time to London again, although intending as well never to leave Bath altogether.

Cheyne and Nash engaged in spirited disputes in Morgan's coffee-house, the outcome of which generally was that the Beau declared his doctor 'the most sensible fool he ever knew'. A sore subject with a mutton-and-chicken epicure like Nash, of course, was Cheyne's diet of vegetables. The Beau maintained that all complaints could be cured by taking the Bath waters inside and out.

'Your design', he accused Cheyne one day at Morgan's 'is to send half the world grazing, like Nebuchadnezzar'.*

'Nebuchadnezzar', retorted the doctor, 'was never such an infidel as thou art. It was but last week, gentlemen, that I attended this fellow in a fit of sickness; there I found him rolling up his eyes to heaven, and crying for mercy; he would then swallow my drugs like breast-milk. Yet you now hear him, how the old dog blasphemes the faculty'.

Whether the portly Cheyne also prescribed gambling for Nash as a restorative is not certain, although such

* And he was driven from men, and did eat grass as oxen. Dan. iv, 33.

advice from the physicians was common at the time. Daniel Defoe now returned (1722) to Bath and cast his observant eye upon the scene of the Assembly: 'The walks behind the Abbey (are) spacious and well shaded, planted all round with shops, filled with everything that contributes to pleasure. At the end is a noble room for gaming, from whence are hanging stairs to a pretty garden for everybody who pays for the time they stay to walk in. We have often wondered that the physicians of these places prescribe gaming to their patients, in order to keep their minds free from business and thought, that their waters on an undisturbed mind may have the greater effect, when indeed one cross throw at play must sour a man's blood more than ten glasses of water will sweeten it'.

He rambled on to look at the bathers: 'The smoke and slime of the waters, the promiscuous multitude of the people in the bath, with nothing but their heads and hands above water, with the height of the walls that environ the bath, gave me a lively idea of several pictures I had seen of Angelo's [Fra Angelico's] in Italy, of Purgatory, with heads and hands uplifted in the midst of smoke, just as they are here'.

But the state of Bath as a whole quite testified to the house-cleaning it had got from Beau Nash: 'Everything looks gay and serene here: it's plentiful and cheap; it's a place of universal sobriety; to be drunk at Bath is as scandalous as mad. Common women are not to be met with here so much as at Tunbridge'. The Master of Ceremonies, of course, paid only fleeting visits to the other place, to the decorum of which he lent relatively minor attention.

It was less of Tunbridge, than of Bath, that the Beau was in the following year, 1723, described as one of the 'characters'. His height, the anonymous writer of a pamphlet said, was five foot eight, to which his 'diameter' was 'exactly proportioned'. The author did not refrain from lyricism: 'Of a black-brown complexion that gives a strength to your looks suited to the elastic force of your nervous fibres and muscles. You have strength and agility to recommend you to your own sex, and great comeliness of person to keep you from being disagreeable to the other. You have heightened a great degree of natural good temper with the greatest politeness, which, improved with your natural good wit, makes your conversation as a private person as entertaining and as delightful, as your authority as a Governor is respectful. With these happy accomplishments, with the fine taste you discover in whatever habit you please to appear, and great gracefulness with which you dance our country dances, it will be no great wonder that you support your Empire when once you obtained it'. Although Nash did not join in the 'French dances', the writer was sure the object of his praise could excel in a minuet as well as in Bartholomy Fair, or in a rigadoon as well as in 'Thomas I Cannot'.

Nevertheless this same writer averred that while Nash was King in Bath, he might be styled Duke at Tunbridge. The distinction was well stated. Tunbridge, for a reason, had appointed no Master of Ceremonies. One Bell Causey, a 'fine but very large woman', formerly in charge of the orange-girls in Hyde Park, was not only the collector of subscriptions at Tunbridge, but 'promoter of friendships' on behalf of the beaux. She stood at the door of the local chapel at the end of morning prayers, buttonholed visitors of rank, and wheedled them into playing host to a large company at a breakfast, a tea-party, a dinner. Entrusted by guests with money for their refreshment, she fed them well, and whatever they left uneaten she gave to the poor. Mrs Causey above all conducted the gaming-room, for which service she earned two guineas a day. Nash for all his prestige was unable to dislodge her from her prerogatives. What he did do was to reinforce at Tunbridge the friendships he had made in Bath, and by opening the season in Tunbridge to render it more fashionable.

In Bath it was admitted that Beau Nash had upheld

'decency and order' in the face of 'play and women'. To keep the throng out of unseemly mischief it was his set scheme to have 'something going on' at every hour of the day. He, individually, ready on the instant to disperse a lull in the excitement, kept the plates spinning with his animation, his anecdote, his glittering diamond snuffbox, to fill up the pauses in the conversation. If he drove home his own jokes without pity, he never took too sensitively the joke of another. Familiar and blunt with his superiors, he eluded their resentment by virtue of his own lower station. They laughed at the same bluntness which his mere equals, who did not matter, complained of as 'insolence'. Sometimes the Master could say rude things with such 'decency' that, by an uncommon turn of phrase, he actually made them pleasing.

It was not so long before that the writer who had called Nash 'Nessus' had spoken as ill of the Beau, the 'common sharper', as the author of the 'Characters' had eulogised him. Perhaps neither writer judged soberly; a just estimate lay somewhere between their views. But the standing of the King of Bath at the moment was certainly in the ascendant, and not least because of the ever-increasing demands for his company as a kind of hydropathic equerry to personages of title.

Of these, Lady Bristol absorbed her full share of attention. She was back in April 1723 with her famous hysterical disorders. Her husband, who seemed so amply endowed with health that he kept aloof from Bath, thought to rally her a little by writing (24 April) that he had received a *billet doux* from the Duchess of Marlborough, now the dowager, and supposedly fond of the Duke of St. Albans, who was at Bath. Lady Bristol answered with spirit, 'If you could see him (the Duke of St. Albans) you would think yourself so very young a man that you would not wonder at your receiving a *billet doux*; but I can't help being peaked enough to mortify your vanity a little by telling you Mr Nash has received one (since I came hither) from the same person'. And on

Frederick, Prince of Wales (1705–51) at the time of his first meeting in Bath (1738) with Beau Nash

Augusta, Princess of Wales (1719–72)

Sarah Porter of Bath, with her 'Subscription Book'. She was taken by Nash in about 1735 to Tunbridge Wells to collect for him at the door of the Ball-room the subscriptions to all Public Entertainments

the subject of invalids she had in the same week to add: 'Poor Bishop Nevell can scarce be reckoned among the living, being (in my opinion) worse than dead; they say he sits at Lindsey's with one to hold his cards and another to give him snuff; palsy and gout have brought him to this miserable condition'. Indeed Lord Bristol must entertain no jealousy: 'Except my Lord Grantham's family', the highly epistolary Countess continued on 1 May, 'there is not a creature that can walk, and the two male kind of them are boys to fill up the set'.

With regard to the great Master of Ceremonies, however, the story was more cheerful; 'I had Mr Nash to dine here' (4 May) 'who has been particularly civil, and more than ordinarily obliging in everything ever since I came; while I kept house he never missed a day coming to enquire how I did'. A week later she was glad to see her Beau restrain the aspiring Grantham family, of whom she was not too fond: 'The Granthams don't succeed so well in their sovereign power over the balls, for though Mr Nash appointed they should not begin last night till 8 a clock (now the weather is warm) yet they would insist upon 7 (since they always retire at 9) and accordingly there are not any French dances above half an hour, and sometimes better, before they could gather five couples together (of creatures) to dance country dances, so that Mr Nash was forced to say aloud, "This dance it will no farther go", for which reason they should have balls but once a week.'

This attempt at social dominance was neither the good Countess's nor Nash's idea of diversion, and within another week Lady Bristol reported: 'The season is so dull that Mr Nash talks every day of leaving us'. It was as well that he did not, for on 19 May the Granthams sought to liven up Bath a bit: 'Illuminations and a large bonfire before Westgate House, where my Lord Grantham lodges; but they were so insolent that when the fire was almost out they broke all the windows in the house; but as the servants knew two of the people Mr Nash said they should produce the rest, and be put in gaol today ... Mr Nash invited me to breakfast.' Nor did this little mêlée deter the good lady on the same evening from launching her daughter Betty on the dancing-floor at the Assembly: 'The most extraordinary thing of all was, Betty, to make the greatest compliments she could to the day, danced four minuets; the first time she trembled, and was so out of countenance I thought she would not have been able to go thro' with it; but the second time she performed very well'.

Upon these laurels Lady Bristol and Betty were content as it were to take holiday from Bath and visit their home. No later than September, however, the Countess was back at the waters, suffering from 'a most extreme lowness of spirits'. Part of her discomfort seemed to arise from witnessing 'seven thousand strangers in Bath', Harrison's turned into Bedlam, and only one person out of a hundred that she had ever seen before. But since that proportion amounted to seventy whom she *had* seen, she was probably able to bear up.

Nash, she found, was as busy as an ant. He was stirring up the whole populace over his great work: the hospital. During this autumn he opened subscriptions. The Master appointed five collectors, of whom himself was one, and armed each with a subscription book. Every likely person in Bath, whether resident or guest, was to be 'touched' for half a guinea or a guinea, and more if it could be squeezed out of a known individual of means. Nash in particular went at the people of title, and Lady Bristol did not escape; from her he extracted three guineas. Her friend the Countess of Orkney gave the same. Three or four other assorted Countesses together yielded to Nash ten guineas. The Duke of St. Albans was good for two. General Wade, lately father-in-law to Ralph Allen, whose wife, Wade's natural daughter, had just died (1722) contributed five guineas: but Allen himself, now doing extremely well as postmaster, made a princely gift of a thousand.

The Beau as a collector employed his wit, his presence of mind, to some effect. A certain man who thought it a nuisance to be asked for a donation exclaimed. 'No, I tell you, no!' Said Nash, 'Just sign here; two negatives make a positive, of course'. Again, Nash encountered in Morgan's coffee-house a close-fisted visitor who was quite irresponsive, and got up to go. 'Remember', Nash called after him, 'if you lose anything on the way home, you didn't draw your purse-strings here'. This was too much; the man turned about, and laid five guineas on the subscription book.

Perhaps the best-known ready subscriber, who after an absence of ten years from Bath turned up early in this September, was Sir Richard Steele. Poor Dick, now fifty-one, wrote to his daughter that he came to the waters with 'a very heavy heart'. In truth he was racked with gout, and he was a bundle of infirmities, no longer acute, as when he had last visited Bath after his election spree, but chronic. His course of immersions must now be no matter of days; he would have to stay for months, in belated repentance for the roystering he could never resist. Steele handed over to Richard Samborne, one of Nash's collectors for the hospital, the odd sum of twenty-seven shillings. The amount sounds as if he gave all he had in his pocket at the time; he never had much, but was generous with what he did possess.

While there is no evidence that the Beau gambled with the funds he gathered in for the hospital, the mere jingle of extra coin in his purse seemed to impel him to the gaming-table for prolonged sittings. To his dismay his luck ran heavily against him, and as if to check himself he determined upon a few days' absence in Bristol, where the Duchess of Marlborough was sojourning. On 14 September he waited upon Lady Bristol, 'to know what commands she had' to that town. But it was the Duchess's commands that he received when he got there. Four days later Lady Bristol advised her husband: 'Play goes on very dully here; bad as it is, poor Nash is almost undone, for 'tis allowed by all that he has lost £1,400 which I believe made him very indifferent company at Bristol. The Duchess wished an appointment with me, and Nash has undertaken it at a half-way house. Lady Orkney, Mr. Nash and myself are the party'.

In time of financial strain, the company of the opulent Sarah Marlborough was no bad elixir. The friendship of the King of Bath and the Queen of Blenheim was ripening.

CHAPTER EIGHT

THE GAMING-TABLE

AS if to appeal to visitors of three generations, or to visitors whose heyday, if not in the present reign, was in the time of either William III or Anne, Beau Nash at the gaming-table 'mixed' in his costume, from about 1725 onward, the dress fashionable under the last two sovereigns with that favoured under George I. Clinging to the kind of elegance in vogue in his youth, he wore a diamond buckle in his stock, as he wore the diamond star to pin back the left flap of his hat. He was loath to give up a full-bottom wig. He affected an expanse of embroidery and frill that had marked the Stuarts. It was mainly in the cut of his clothes that he followed the Hanoverians.

Not even his loss of £1,400 impaired his prestige as guardian of the games. His net reputation was that he was a winner, because of his 'superior skill and dispassionate attention'. Players who lost £20 to £200 begged Nash to tie them up, like Ulysses, lest they succumb to the siren sound of the dice, and the Master often caught hold of a player's dice-box in mid-air. Sometimes he intervened by indirection: he once employed a sharper to win all the money of a young bridegroom. The victim rushed out mad. 'No!' cried his bride, overtaking him with the funds. 'Mr Nash has saved us both'.

Not always did he succeed in dissuading these amateurs from play prolonged to recklessness. It was in this year of 1725 that a young Oxford don, contrary to the usual way of his kind, resigned his fellowship and brought with him to Bath all the money he possessed. With no knowledge of gambling he encountered beginner's luck, and soon added £4,000 to his capital, some of which gains he won from Nash himself. The Beau invited him to supper in St. John's Court, not to take 'revenge' under his own roof, but to give counsel.

'You are now high in spirits', he reminded his guest, 'and drawn away by a torrent of success. But there will come a time when you will repent having left the calm of a college life . . . Ill runs will come . . . remain content with your present gains . . . Had you the Bank of England, with your present ignorance of gaming, it would vanish . . . I'll give you fifty guineas, to forfeit twenty, every time you lose 200 at a sitting'.

The young scholar refused. He went back to Harrison's and in no great time fulfilled the Master's prophecy. The 'ill runs' overtook him, and ran relentlessly. He fled Bath penniless. He was heard of no more.

Not always was the intervention of Nash in the lives of his visitors either so brief or so ineffectual. It might extend over years, and yield its reward at last. In one case it involved the use of his carriage. This vehicle, necessary especially to transport him between Bath and Tunbridge, was as resplendent as a Lord Mayor's coach. The sun picked out the chariot of Nash to shine upon as it hummed through the town, drawn by six greys and turreted by lackeys with apple cheeks blowing into French horns. There was a running footman as well, Bryan, a burly Irishman, who accompanied the Master on journeys to Tunbridge, or to points farther afield, such as Peterborough, whither the coach had to travel near this time.

The occasion had to do with a love affair, begun some years before in Bath, between a certain impecunious Colonel and a lady whose rich father wished her to marry a certain nobleman. The Colonel would have carried off his bride had not Nash apprised the father, who promptly recalled his daughter from Bath. While the old gentleman was appreciative to the point of offering Nash a handsome gift, which the Master declined, the Colonel, discovering the hitch, challenged the 'informer' to a duel. This, Nash also declined. Not only did he prohibit swords in Bath; he was aware that he had saved the young lady from being disinherited, and saved both herself and the Colonel from misery. Thereupon the Colonel determined to engage Nash in combat as soon as he should come to London. But the Colonel's creditors now pressed him so hard that he could escape them only by going overseas; he joined the Dutch army in Flanders.

The nobleman now pursued his advantage. Nor did the lady reject his addresses, since the Colonel rather became a matter of 'out of sight, out of mind'. Her father then died, leaving her £1,500 a year. The nobleman had almost persuaded the lady to forget the Colonel when Nash, hearing of the father's death, made diligent enquiry after the absent soldier, found that he had returned to England, had changed his name to elude his creditors, and joined a company of actors who were playing in Peterborough.

The Master invited the lady and her suitor to make a party, in his gilded coach, on a drive thither. They all went to the play, which was Dick Steele's last comedy, *The Conscious Lovers*, popular ever since its opening in 1722. Nash took seats in the front row, placing the lady between himself and the nobleman. The Colonel was appearing in the minor and rascally part of Tom, servant to young Bevil. But as soon as he came on, in the first scene, for his dialogue with the old servant Humphry, he recognised his beloved, who at sight of him fainted away. The Colonel, unable to speak his lines, leapt down from the stage and caught her in his arms.

'Colonel!' cried Nash. 'If you love well enough now for matrimony, you fairly have my consent, and damn him, say I, that attempts to part you'.

That was the last of the nobleman; and the wedding of the lovers followed almost as soon as their reuniter had got back to Bath.

While it could not be said that the gambling at Bath was responsible for reducing the Colonel to penury, for he was extravagant wherever he was, play was now in so many instances working havoc amongst those who could not afford to lose, that a satirical comedy, *The Bath Unmasked*, by Gabriel Odingsells, performed at Lincoln's Inn Fields in February 1725, bore some resemblance to fact. Prominent in its cast was John Hippisley, as Sir Captious Whiffle. But the typical scene was the opening of Act IV, discovering Lady Ambs-Ace rising from a table in a fury, whilst the sharpers divided her money.

First Sharper: I profess we would not refuse your Ladyship a few pieces; but cash runs low at this time—and this is such an iron age that a gentleman has a villainous time of it to live upon credit. Your Ladyship cannot want money. Whenever you are prepared we will give you your revenge.   [*Exit sharpers*].

Lady A: Get you gone for a set of bloodhounds! Quite stript! Yet here are my deities [*takes up dice*] though I have no sacrifice to offer them. Fame and fortune ye have had already; my hourly prayers ye have, though ye requite me ill. Yet such is the power of your charms that rather than want offerings for you I'll keep a set of bravos in pay, who shall cut throats and rob altars to adorn your shrine.

There were other scenes in Harrison's gardens, Harrison's long room, the Grove, before the Abbey, and in various lodgings. The author's opinion of the ladies in general at Bath he expressed in these lines between Pander and Sprightly:

Pander: As for ladies, we have of all degrees, as their several interests draw 'em hither. Those of the first rank—

Sprightly: Who have too much honour to keep an honourable vow.

Pander: That's your own comment—I say, who

understand the use of nature better than to be confined to conjugal constancy, improve their talents by private intercourse; coquettes enlarge their conquests; prudes indulge in a corner, and are demure in public (though thanks to spreading libertinism, that class decreases daily); professed ladies of pleasure find cullies in abundance.

Yet the actual season ensuing did not seem to bear out that Bath was altogether a den of vice. The merry Molly Lepel, Lady Hervey, wrote to Henrietta Howard in June of the well-conducted pleasures of baronets or sons of lords, men who gave breakfasts for fifty or sixty people. Nor did Molly miss the humour in the eccentric Lord Peterborough, who defied Nash's rule against the boots, wore them all day, and even in his blue ribbon and star went to market, whence he returned with a cabbage under each arm and swinging a chicken. And in the early autumn Lady Hervey was again at the waters, to report of 'many private balls' addressed to Lady Walsingham. This tall plain youngish German lady, Melusina de Schulenbergh, who still said 'd' for 'th', was a bastard of the King by his mistress the Duchess of Kendall. But for nearly a month in September and October she 'made' the season at Bath, while for the Master of Ceremonies she made reputation. Lady Walsingham was Nash's nearest approach to royalty since he had staged his pageant in London for William III—a whole generation gone by—and he made the most of his renewed opportunities. Accelerating the pace of the diversions at Bath, he let no moment sag for Lady Walsingham. If the story of his capability as a host was to reach St. James's Palace, she was the messenger.

Yet the Beau was in other ways no respecter of persons. He was a Samaritan; he did good for its own sake; and sometimes he did good in spite of himself. Guests and local people alike were beginning to see that Mr Nash was too complex to be defined; no sooner had they thought they knew his dimensions than he either extended or rectified their lines. It was in 1726 that a poor vicar, who had to keep a wife and a vicar's usual litter of six children on a living of £30 a year, brought his family to Bath. His wife was suffering from a malady which it was believed nothing but the waters would alleviate. So long had her treatment dragged on that the vicar had now to sell his clothes, piece by piece, in order to live. The things he still kept—his coat, his stockings—began to show so many holes that Nash, in the unkindly jocose way he sometimes affected, took to referring to the hapless man as Doctor Cullender.

The vicar, instead of complaining, or begging, tried to conceal his hardships, even in the face of having to let his family go hungry. At last, when he had nothing left, someone reported the true circumstances to the Master of Ceremonies. Nash then undertook a ceremony that showed how far he deserved his title and office: of a Sunday evening—the day being well chosen because the question appertained to a clergyman—the Beau attended a public tea-drinking at Harrison's. He went about collecting a fund in aid, which he opened with five guineas of his own. In less than two hours he gathered 200 guineas.

Not medicines, but the money, cured the vicar's wife, by the remedial power of joy. Meanwhile Nash persuaded a nobleman whom he knew, and who had in his gift a living worth £160, to appoint this vicar. Never were those who imagined that the Master reserved his attentions for the great worse confounded.

He looked after the humanities of Bath, as Ralph Allen and his father-in-law General Wade were turning their energies rather upon its amenities. Allen as postmaster and Wade as M.P. for Bath were intent upon improving conditions both within the town and in its outlying districts. Allen, running the post-office from the nave of an old church, wished to expedite the mails, and to this end Wade collaborated in 1726 by employing soldiers to lay down 'highland roads'. In Bath itself Wade at his own expense helped the post-office by clearing slums impinging upon it, slums whose inhabitants terrorised the postal staff. The General contributed to many local charities, not the least of them the hospital which Nash was still forwarding for the poor. While the Beau at no time worked with Allen and Wade as a committee, their common purpose lent strength to the efforts of each.

But it was to individuals, in great variety, local or visiting, that Nash devoted most of his time. Dr Cheyne, for example, the man who came to Bath weighing thirty-two stone, but who wrote a book called *Health and Long Life*, was one whom the Master as a matter of habit ridiculed to his face and admired behind his back. And Cheyne whether at Morgan's or elsewhere gave Nash as good as he sent. Knowing that the Beau was addicted to late suppers, after which he went to bed, Cheyne taunted him:

'You behave like other brutes, and lie down as soon as you have filled you belly.'

'Very true', retorted Nash, 'and that prescription I had from my neighbour's cow, who is a better physician than you, and a superior judge of plants, notwithstanding you have written so learnedly on the vegetable diet'.

None of this badinage caused Nash to restrain Molly Lepel's husband, the valetudinarian Lord Hervey, from visiting Dr Cheyne. Joining his wife in Bath in 1726, Hervey was a wraith of a man whose London physicians had been giving him ass's milk with powdered crab's eyes and oyster-shells. This diet hardly offset the meat and wine to which he was accustomed. Cheyne put Hervey on nothing but cow's milk for two months, to be followed solely by 'roots, fruits, herbs and pulse' for three years. The invalid seemed to gain strength from the mere prospect.

It was of course not those who came for health, but those in pursuit of 'wealth' that were likely to make trouble for the King of Bath. The part that Nash the perennial bachelor had to play as referee in affairs of the heart did not always bear so happy an outcome as in the case of the lady, the soldier, and the nobleman. The dramatic scene at Peterborough was sometimes surpassed, and with an unfortunate aftermath, for all that the Beau could do to intervene.

It was in 1726 that Miss Fanny Braddock, aged nineteen, appeared in Bath, probably not for the first time. She was of a military family, her father, Edward Braddock, having served with the Coldstream in Flanders and Spain, and his namesake, her brother, being at present a lieutenant in the same regiment. The elder Braddock died in Bath in 1720, with the rank of major-general, and was buried in the Abbey Church. He left his daughter about £10,000. She was attractive, gay, sought after, but discontented that her income did not allow her yet more gaiety than she already enjoyed. To replenish her purse, she resolved upon gaming at Bath.

Her admirers increased faster than her resources. This might have proved no bad thing, for in choosing from those who professed their love she stood at least as good a chance as the heiress pursued by the soldier and the nobleman. But her popularity led her to suppose she could defer her decision for the mere fun of the game, also that when she did give her heart she could not possibly bestow it upon the wrong man. If there was anything wrong about him, she could in her wisdom make it right.

No suitor prevailed until a philanderer and a spendthrift called 'Mr S.' turned up at the tables. He was a character not unfamiliar in Bath, where he was known to many who had nothing to lose from his blithe companionship as 'the good-natured man'. Whatever money he could get he spent either upon a woman or upon a drinking companion. Fanny Braddock soon showed that she enjoyed S's frivolities more than she valued the ardour of his rivals. Nash warned her, others warned her, that the affection of S. was about as constant as that of a sailor; but like many a girl not come of age Fanny only resented their 'interference'. She redoubled her responses to the man.

At length S. left Bath, and the affair seemed to fall into abeyance. But he left only to run into serious trouble with his creditors. They gaoled him for debt. He was not one to whine; he tried to prevent Miss Braddock from hearing about it. But she found means of discovering his whereabouts, and as soon as she did, she told those who had tried to dissuade her from pursuing this butterfly that she was resolved to buy him out of detention.

Nash was in London at the time. All the Braddocks in town, who could do nothing with Fanny, begged the Beau to stop her from throwing her money away. He had a talk with the girl. He told her that so large a reduction in her fortune would not only make her less desirable in the eyes of other men, but that it would make her less esteemed even by the women. Though delivered from gaol, said Nash, the 'good-natured man' would never work to repay her, for there was no substance to his affection; on the contrary, he would seek to elude a single creditor so large. 'Small favours make good-will', concluded the Beau. 'Great ones destroy friendship'.

The firmness of purpose characteristic of Fanny Braddock was not to be shaken. She took no more notice of Nash's importunity than she had taken of her family's, or of that of her friends in Bath in the first instance. She paid the man's debts. He fled from the gaol like a bird from a cage, and this time she failed to find him again.

CHAPTER NINE

JOHN WOOD

IN 1727 a young man of twenty-two called John Wood came to Bath to live, and to practise as an architect. It was no sudden decision that he made; he had been thinking over this move for three years. Early aware of Acts of Parliament under which the roads leading into Bath were to be improved, and the Avon made navigable from Bristol up to Bath, Wood had got a plan of Bath sent to him in Yorkshire, and there he worked out designs for the northeast and the northwest sections of the town. The first he took to London in 1725 to show to Dr Gay, the principal landowner, and the second he presented in the following year to the Earl of Essex, landlord of that part.

Young Wood was a 'man of vision'. He built air castles up and down streets yet unmarked. He was possessed with the spirit of ancient Rome, with a sense of magnificence. He saw spread before him 'a grand Place of Assembly, to be called the Royal Forum of Bath'; he saw a mammoth edifice for 'the exhibition of Sports, to be called the Grand Circus'; he saw a great building 'for the Practice of Medicinal Exercises', to be called the 'Imperial Gymnasium'. Most exuberant of all, he saw himself as the man destined to bring these monuments into being.

Lord Essex and Dr Gay listened to Wood's raptures, but did not envisage much profit arising from forums and circuses. Nor yet did they drive the lad dejectedly back into Yorkshire. From their reception of his enthusiasm Wood derived enough encouragement to proceed to Bath, settle, and see what he could do, on a scale somewhat less grandiose, about rebuilding the town.

It was in May that Wood, his 'engagements in London drawing to a period', came to Bath, only to be 'zealously' beset by Dame Lindsey to build her a house. He could hardly have avoided meeting Beau Nash at the same time, since the Dame was an employee of the Master. Wood is said to have been odd-looking. The upper part of his face was handsome, with great dark Spanish eyes, arched brows, and the nose of a patrician, long and cleancut; but he was disfigured by thick lips, and although he wore a little goatee he appeared to have swallowed his chin. Freak he may have looked; but he was to get his chance to prove himself an artist. He was indeed a man of ideas. These ideas might not always gain acceptance, as in the case of Gay and Essex; but even if unworkable the mere suggesting of them got John Wood a hearing.

It was enough to win the interest of Nash for him that Wood, soon after his arrival in this year of 1727, proposed that the new Hospital be built in Ambery Mead, a vegetable garden near the Hot Spring, for the advantageous reason that a bath could then be piped into the middle. But those who hesitated, over the purchase of this site, lost. Someone else bought the Mead.

Yet Wood had more than enough schemes in his head to suffer overmuch from the hesitations of others. In 1728 he began excavating, to the greater glory of Nash and Dame Lindsey alike, for new Assembly-rooms, nearly opposite the older building. Here he struck the ancient burial-ground of a monastery; one of his workmen grew opulent from selling the teeth and bones of horses as relics of gigantic prehistoric man. In the same year Wood began to lay out the North and South Parades, comprehending old Ham Gardens, the walls of which had long served as a 'back-drop' for the Chartered Fair of Bath. The gardens themselves had from time immemorial produced 'black cluster' grapes, which yielded the famous wine of Bath; but the crops were now beginning to fail.

Wood had a grandiose dream for this site, with hundreds of Corinthian columns facing a square, and in the centre an immense ballroom. If Lord Essex and Dr Gay had thwarted his plans for their property, Wood was simply plunging ahead elsewhere. At the end of the year he broke further ground for Queen's Square, 500 feet to a side, each side to look like a Corinthian palace. The North façade, with its mid-section suggestive of the Parthenon, was the first to rise.

Whilst Wood was thus embellishing Bath, Nash as Master of Ceremonies was heightening its prestige. In this busy year of 1728 the most eminent visitor was the new King's daughter, Princess Amelia. The Beau sent forth, to escort her from the boundary of Somerset through the north Gate, the triumphal arch of Bath, a hundred armed young men in uniform. He received her at her lodgings in Broad Street. In her German way she was comely enough, with her fuzzy hair, and in a great bell-shaped hat from which depended a scarf gathered at the chin. Her blue eyes looked milder than her character was known to be. People were in awe of the Princess. At Tunbridge, where she had just been a sojourner, Lord Boyle said: 'If she laughs (and sometimes Princesses laugh at nothing) we all grin. If she looks grave, we put on countenances sorrier than the mutes at a funeral. When she walks, the lame and the blind hobble after her. If she complains of the toothache, the ugly faces of the women of quality are wrapped up in flannel'. Was her Royal Highness now to cast a similar spell upon Nash's citadel of Bath? At seventeen she was inclined to tattle, she was mischievous, and sometimes insolent, although she could be kind, generous, and steady in friendship. People awesomely called her 'a character'. She loved cards, went hunting dressed like a man, and ate her breakfast standing up.

The princess attended the ball, and she danced the evening through, through the last country-dance. At eleven o'clock the musicians ceased playing. But Amelia wished to go on.

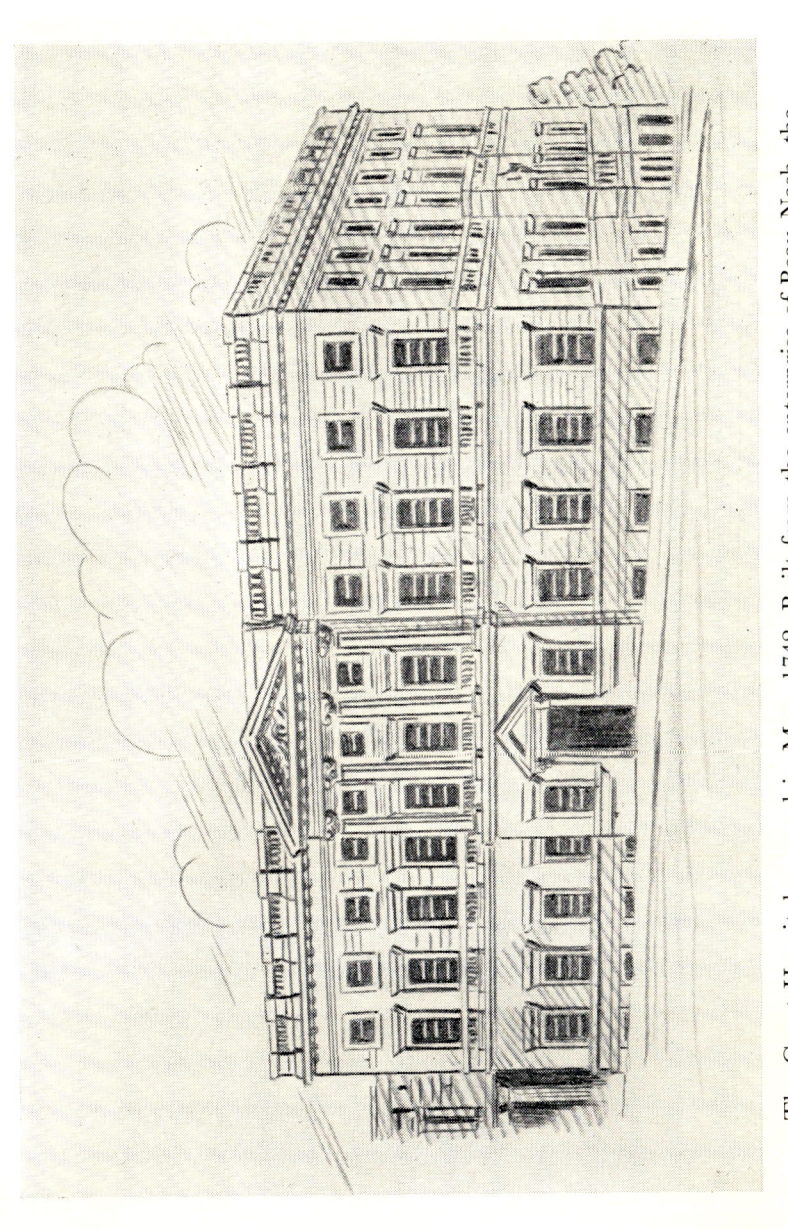

The Great Hospital, opened in May, 1742. Built from the enterprise of Beau Nash, the quarry of Ralph Allen, and the plans of John Wood

The Pantiles, Tunbridge Wells, in August, 1748. Beau Nash (centre, in black wig) is walking with Elizabeth Chudleigh (1720–88) and William Pitt (1708–88), Paymaster-General, later Earl of Chatham

[The 'Dr. Johnson', at the left with the Bishop of Salisbury, is believed to be James Johnson, D.D. (1705–74) chaplain to George II.]

'One more dance, Mr Nash!' she requested.

The Beau looked at her in astonishment.

'Remember,' she rallied him, 'I am a Princess'.

'Yes, Madam', he returned. 'But I reign here. The laws of Bath are as changeless as the laws of Lycurgus. To break them once would break down all their authority'.

The Princess, with good grace, subsided.

When she left Bath, she presented the Master with a silver tureen.

It was in compliment as well as to the town as to Nash that she made the gift. Bath under the transforming hand of John Wood was a memorable sight. Not only were the great blocks of new buildings going up in classic dimensions to dominate the razed squares; Wood was also designing, for individuals, private houses on lines equally arresting. One of them was for Ralph Allen, who had now so prospered in his management of the post-office that he was able to move from his quarters in the nave of the old church against the slums.

The house for Allen was in Lilliput Alley, behind York Street, in a new part of the North Parade passage. The Alley was already distinguished by the cake shop of Sally Lunn, who night and morning carried about in a basket her hot buttered tea-cakes. That these cakes were driving other delicacies of the kind off the market appeared from the quatrain:

> No more I heed the muffin's zest,
>   The Yorkshire cake or bun;
> Sweet Muse of Pastry! teach me how
>   To make a Sally Lunn.

Wood so situated Allen's house—to which the postmaster took his second bride, Elizabeth Holder, of Hampton Manor—that it faced sloping gardens, and thence a view of hills beyond. The front of this house rose proudly in four Corinthian columns, which bore fruit and flowers above them. To conform with the great squares, Queen's and the Parade, the columnar bases in the new house rested upon the first floor above the ground, while in wings jutting to right and left Allen was to accommodate his post-office staff. So through the collaboration of Allen and Wood came artistry into the postal service of Bath, as through Nash came decorum amongst its visitors. In singleness of purpose, the greater glory of the town, the three men were a constructive triumvirate.

What John Wood sagaciously foresaw was that he ran no risk of overbuilding. In popularity and in fashion Bath grew and grew, attracting all classes, both as a resort and as a cure. The people of title were becoming resigned to the mixed company. 'For my own part', Lady Anne Irwin in September 1729 told Lord Carlisle, 'I think it no great difference whether 'tis a crowd of quality or plebeians'. Yet she had no love of a crowd of any kind: 'Harrison's rooms are so full every night 'tis to me very disagreeable; if one had an inclination to play, 'tis next to impossible to get a table to play.'

But now the new Assembly-room in Terrace Walk was about to relieve the congestion. If it was built upon hallowed ground, the burying was so far in the dim past that none was disturbed by the sacrilege. Workmen displaced coffins hewn out of a single stone, bones encased in hides, with shoes, or leathern shrouds without shoes. The hidebound were probably monks, the stone-encased either Saxons or Romans. And now John Wood's palace of pleasure, which he had built by direction of one Humphrey Thayer, rose above the field of eternity. It was to be called Thayer's Assembly-room. In form it was a double cube, thirty feet to a side. The Friday evening ball was to be transferred to it from Harrison's, thus dividing the throng, and allowing them more room to gamble.

Harrison shifted Dame Lindsey, his onetime opera-singer who was doing so well after forsaking Tunbridge for Bath, to Thayer's as manager, on the understanding that she operate the new Rooms at lower cost to the public. Patrons had long complained of the excessive charges at Harrison's. To this appointment of Mrs Lindsey the

Master of Ceremonies agreed; with her he became associated in the new supervision. Early in 1730 Thayer's opened its doors.

Soon afterward Fanny Braddock, urged by Nash, reappeared in Bath. She was now twenty-three. The years immediately subsequent to her folly of paying the debts of her 'good-natured man', her 'man of great heart', had proved in London doubly painful to her. That man had not vanished for long. He materialised, whirling about in another sea of debt; he was apprehended, he was gaoled, and he died in gaol. Fanny was shorn of all but a trifle of her fortune, with the result that her family shut her out and her friends put her off, all except the King of Bath, who although Miss Braddock had ignored his warning still desired to help her. He believed that in view of her charm and her social capability he might, by introducing her to ladies of means and influence, expose her to enough sense to cause her to absorb some of it.

The great ladies to whom the Beau appealed made considerable effort on Fanny's behalf. With some reason, they suspected that she was still marriageable. Unhappily such amusements in Bath as were harmless failed to cheer the young lady. She was a gambler, even without knowing how to gamble; and she appeared to be irredeemable. At the tables she lost such funds as she had left.

Dame Lindsey, unscrupulous as she was, had been keeping a calculative eye upon this young woman. Now quite penniless, Fanny was malleable, and when the Dame, concluding that she could make use of her, offered her employment as a decoy, Fanny for lack of any other means of living accepted that shady occupation. At this turn the ladies who had been trying to help her ceased trying.

Yet the character of Miss Braddock rested in other particulars above reproach. As soon as her guardian Nash discovered what Lindsey had done he intervened, fully aware that a young miss in the clutches of the Dame was bound to lose caste. The Beau clung to his determination to establish Fanny reputably. He besought John Wood to take her into his house as governess. Wood was willing; but Miss Braddock, who had begun almost to enjoy luring the unwary to the dice-box, had to be persuaded to go. Had it not been for her fondness of Nash, and her acknowledgement of him as her confessor—some later said the Beau had been one of her lovers—she would have refused to give up the excitement of the Assembly-rooms. In the end Fanny agreed to take charge of the children in question; she moved into the house of the architect in Queen's Square.

Nash reckoned he had now placed his 'ward', at least for the time being, not only at a safe distance from the scene of hazard, but under responsible protection. While he may well have heard that Miss Braddock as cheerful companion to a family gave little promise, he was too wrapped up in his manifold duties to keep her continually in mind. For one thing, the great scheme of the Hospital was absorbing him. By the spring of this year, April 1731, he and his colleagues had collected (apart from Allen's special gift) £330; it was but a start toward the £2,500 they estimated for the building and beds, yet the sum was adequate to justify the appointing of trustees, men of repute whose names alone would draw further contributions. And there was another incentive, new and glowing; Robert Gay promised to convey the land needed. The men behind the scheme now envisaged the Hospital already standing, even healing its inmates.

Its trustees included Nash himself, him above all; then the Mayor, two Justices, and two Aldermen of Bath; the list ended with Ralph Allen, Dr Cheyne, Dr William Oliver (inventor of 'Bath Olivers'), and Humphrey Thayer. As Thayer actually lived in Hatton Garden, he was expected to look after the London side of the subscriptions. So little doubt did these gentlemen entertain of eventually gathering the funds required that they proceeded to draw up 'articles', under which patients from outlying parishes were to be admitted to the amenities in prospect. These plans they laid open to the scrutiny of every potential contributor to the cause.

During the summer succeeding, Fanny Braddock managed to perform her stated tutelage in the house of John Wood. But she grew into a solitary. Word spread that she changed her housemaid's name to Nash, as if for an excuse always to have the name of her friend upon her lips. In London they had been together; in Bath they were separated. Her incarceration, shut off as she was from the hum and the commotion at Thayer's; her dependence, now that her fortune was gone; and the harassment of children who stirred in her more irritation than self-effacement, at length tended to aggravate her depressed state of mind. She had contrived her own penury. She lacked the courage to earn her way out of it. As life, she was sure, held in store for her nothing more, she resolved to do away with herself.

On the night of 4 September 1731 her employer John Wood was absent in London. Fanny, having put her charges to bed, tried to divert herself with Ariosto's *Orlando Furioso;* but the passage that caught her eye was the one which dealt with the unfortunate end of Olympia. Far from causing the governess to hesitate, this episode deepened her resolution. She put on her nightgown, and taking a gold-and-silver girdle, tied near an end of it three knots, about an inch apart, lest one of them slip. At the other end of the girdle she fastened a noose. Standing on a chair near the door, she tossed the knotted end over the door, which she then locked, and its key she clasped in her hand. Finally she kicked away the chair.

When her brother, Lieutenant Edward Braddock, heard in London of the suicide, he only remarked, 'Poor Fanny! I always thought she would play till she would be forced to tuck *herself* up!'

CHAPTER TEN

A CURIOSITY FROM HOLLAND

THE callous jest of Fanny Braddock's brother turned upon the actual phrase used in Bath to safeguard a losing gambler from dicing until he lost all he possessed. He either asked to be 'tied up' or he was urged by others to let himself be tied up. The young Duke of Bolton, who in 1722 had come into his estates at thirty-seven, began, with the usual result, to appear too frequently at the tables. Losing, he besought Nash to 'tie him up' from plunging. The Master in compliance gave Bolton a hundred guineas, to forfeit ten thousand whenever he lost at one sitting the same amount from play.

Not very long after the two had entered into this agreement, the Duke, at his beloved tables, found that he was down £8,000. He made as if to throw for another £3,000. Nash caught hold of the dice-box, reminding him of what was at stake. For once, Bolton left off. He thus saved Bath and Nash from further ill report—in Bath.

Unhappily in October 1731 (within a month after the death of Fanny Braddock) the Duke took his gambling to Newmarket. The agreement between him and Nash applied not to Bath alone, but to gambling anywhere. Bolton, losing at the races a sum beyond the limit set, now had to pay the Beau, just as if the loss had occurred in the Assembly-rooms. If Nash was shaken by two crises so close together, he at least suffered no later trouble from either source.

While the suicide of Fanny, if not the recklessness of Bolton, for some time left its mark upon the Master of

Ceremonies, not all who observed him fathomed the cause of his sadness. On 3 November Lord Orrery proffered his conjectures to Lady Kaye: 'Nash seems dejected, and oppressed at heart; I suppose he has not yet recovered his losses of last year, and the malicious part of us say that his taxes and contributions are much lessened, and that upon his application to his Parliament' (the Bath Town Council or Corporation) 'for a vote of credit, the majority was against it. What, Madam, can be more abject than a despised King? He seems to labour under the unconquerable distemper of old age, and though he attends the balls as usual, his dancing days are over'. To him, Nash was dying at fifty-seven.

But the question of 'old age' seemed to obsess Lord Orrery, as if he had come to Bath to make a study of senility. Only a fortnight later he was writing to Councillor Kempe: 'Since my coming to Bath I am perfectly convinced that the ancient patriots were a thoughtless race of people, who loved country dances, and breakfast on hot rolls and butter. They lived to an immense length of days merely by leading the same kind of life that is prevalent at this place, where the Methusalems and the Abrahams dance with as much vigour at the balls as if they had flourished in a courant at Charles the Second's restoration.

'To be more particular; Here is a Brocas (now in his 97th year *currente anno*) who avers he never was sick in his life, nor ever paid a groat for a pennyworth of physick, which athletic constitution he attributes to an utter inattention either to the cares of the public or the various fortunes of his private friends . . . He is at Bath in May, at Tunbridge in July, at Bath again in September . . . The pale-faced girls are all fond of him, and they are sure to be well tousled when he leads up the kissing dance. Do not imagine from hence that he is a dangerous or a poisonous animal . . . Mothers trust him alone with their daughters in the dark . . . the married woman takes his advice in laces and tippets. Some envious persons call him a dangler ... But his patience surmounts and baffles all brutalities by a grave grin that at once denotes inward satisfaction and outward philosophy.

'We have here an Ingram "who whistles as he goes for want of thought". He is an old Brobdingnagian, or rather a Struldbrug of the first magnitude. Yet the ladies, notwithstanding his dreadful aspect, are grown familiar with often seeing him, and will venture to romp with him as if he were no bigger than a monkey.

'Here are antidiluvians of lesser note and fewer years. A Brigadier Warren who is forced to make use of a cane in his 79th year. Here is also one Dockry, a moneylender, and one Laydeman of the same tread; but these are looked upon as really immortal, being true sons of Mammon in human shapes. Here is a Mr Pitt with a swinging cane, and two eyes looking each a different way; here are also many lords, pickpockets, broken merchants, and disconsolate widows. There wants only a Sandford to complete our group'.

If in this group the 'decrepit' Nash was included, he was not yet so far gone but that he had his uses. A chef, a composer, and a highwayman dedicated their books to him, and 'many a versifier so saved himself from a bailiff'. Nash thirsted for praise, even from a highwayman. This bandit, one Baxter, dating his book from Taunton gaol, exposed the tricks of thieves and gamblers, and said: 'As your Honour's wisdom, humanity, and interest are the friend of the virtuous, I make bold to lay at your Honour's feet the following work'. The composer enquired: 'To whom should I presume to offer these, my first attempts at musical composition, but to the great encourager of all polite arts?' He went on with much more: generosity, dignity, grace, humanity, and beneficience. The chef, in his dedication, burst into simile, and not of the kitchen: 'As much as the oak exceeds the bramble, so do you, honoured Sir, exceed the rest of mankind in benevolence, charity, and every other virtue that adorns, ennobles, and refines the human species'.

It was within the echo of such salutes that the Beau in 1732 was driving his six grey coach-horses to Tunbridge, horses 'so well matched and paced so well together when in full trot that any person at a distance would imagine it was only one horse that drew the carriage'. This pomp (for an excursion outside Bath) embraced besides a coachman and a postillion two footmen, a show of outriders and French horns, a gentleman 'out of livery', and Bryan, the tireless Irish running-footman.

On the present glistening occasion the Master really hoped to make a start in 'developing' Tunbridge. One morning on the Pantiles he and a friend fell in with a young man of means whom they knew slightly, and joined him. Nash asked him how long he had been at the Wells, and what company he had found.

'A month', replied the young blade. 'But as for company, I can find as good at a Tyburn ball. Not a soul is to be seen, except a parcel of gamesters, and whores who will grant the last favour for a single stake at the farobank. Look you there, that goddess of midnight, so fine, at t'other end of the walks, by Jove, she was mine this morning for half a guinea. And she, there, who brings up the rear with powdered hair and dirty ruffles: she's pretty enough, but cheap, perfectly cheap. Why, my boys, to my own knowledge, you may have her for a crown, and a dish of chocolate into the bargain. Last Wednesday night we were happy'.

Nash's friend interrupted him.

'As for your having the first lady, it is possible it may be true, and I intend to ask her about it, for she is my sister. But as for your lying with the other last Wednesday, I am sure you are a lying rascal. She is my wife, and we came here but last night'.

It was not enough that the younger man asked pardon. Nash's friend was about to thrash him. But the Master interposed, and gained the consent of his friend to let the offender off on condition that he quit Tunbridge forthwith.

There ended, for the time, the 'developing' of the resort by Nash. His interference angered Bell Causey.

Nash did not long tarry. There was always too much to supervise at Bath. For some twenty-five years now, the old Pump-room had served its purpose but too well. It almost bulged with the crowds. In this year it was being pulled down, and a larger one on the same site substituted, twenty-six by forty-three feet. The new design was to include two refinements indicative of the elegance to which Nash devoted himself: a gallery for the musicians, and a marble cistern to replace the lead one, which was considered perhaps less appetising to the imbibing invalids.

The new building was well timed, for the event of the season was a return visit by the Princess Amelia, the exacting eccentric. She resumed her lodgings in her 'mansion' in Broad Street, and in celebration of her coming a sheet of verses was inscribed to her:

> Where the smooth bowl was wont to skim the green,
> Now stately rooms for pleasure change the scene;
> Where music warbles, and the dancers bound,
> While the high roof re-echoes to the sound;
> There blooming virgins kindle wondrous fires,
> And there the god of art with verse inspires.
> The rattling dye enchants the anxious heir;
> The hoarded sums the sharking gamesters share.
> The important business of the fair—quadrille,
> Employs those hours which dancing cannot kill;
> Or fav'rite ombre, sweetly sung by Pope,
> Appals their cheeks with fear, or reddens them with hope.
> There miss soon learns the language of the eyes;
> The witless beau looks soft, and swears he dies,
> And who can think so fine a lover lies?
> There pagan, Turk, the Papist and the Jew,
> And all mankind's epitome you view.

While it may be questioned in what respect this effusion paid homage to the Princess, its lines upon the dancing and the gambling, not to mention the rest, may have reminded her of the diversions she had come to seek.

The presence of a Princess, or other personages of mark,

made ambitious mothers all the more solicitous to see that their daughters danced with the 'right people'. Upon one occasion, such a lady asked the Master to get a partner for a daughter of hers, and when Nash complied, the daughter danced through the whole evening with this man. On the next day, in the Pump-room, a busybody informed the mother that the man was a linen-draper from Cheapside.

The lady complained rather bitterly to the Beau.

There were times when in a social way Nash had to think quickly. 'Yes, madam', he explained. 'Your daughter's partner does deal in linen. But it is on the wholesale side. He never *cut* a piece of linen in his life'.

The indignant mother was mollified.

Beau Nash was a kind of protean Samaritan, of broadly philanthropic heart. Whether the dejection of an individual in Bath was social, bodily, or financial, Nash always wanted to do his utmost to relieve it, at whatever the cost to himself. It was his skill and impassiveness at the gaming-table that enabled him to support the material end of this charity. One evening a player whose fortune had ebbed away was standing behind the Beau, who was casually engaging in picquet for £200. This he won with indifference.

'Heavens!' whispered the man to a bystander, 'how happy would all that money make me!'

Nash, on the spur, may have recalled the incident of the impoverished man in the Temple, a generation before, to whom he gave ten pounds, and charged it to the benchers 'for making a man happy'. Now, overhearing behind him the man in like case, he put the £200 into his hands, and simply said, 'Go and be happy'.

A time in which he was able to make so kingly a gesture was a time in which he was prepared to welcome a Prince. Toward the middle 1730's, it has been observed, not only was Nash's word law, but his bow was an honour, and his acquaintance was a passport to the best circles. In 1734 the Prince of Orange journeyed to Bath for the waters. Like Richard III, he was 'deformed, unfinished, scarce half made up'. Lord Hervey went further, and said the Prince 'looked behind as if he had no head, and in front as if without neck or legs'. But the Prince was a good man, and kindly. Upon his marrying a daughter of George II, the Princess Royal, the Princess had boldly said: 'if he was a *monkey* I would have him'. The looks of the man of course made no difference to Beau Nash, who was used to receiving many an oddly-shaped invalid. The point was that Bath was now enhanced by the patronage of Nash's first prince, and so was Nash.

The diminutive Prince attended by the gigantic Master of Ceremonies were a strange pair at the baths and in the Pump-room. But the Prince so assiduously followed the regimen laid down that he regained much of his vigour, such as it was, and in gratitude to the Beau he presented him with a handsome snuff-box, jewelled.

This was no ordinary gift. The recipient, to emphasise the honour, not to say to focus attention upon his own eminence, let it be known that the Prince's snuff-box was to be the start of a collection of them by the Master. The subtle invitation bore the expected fruit. As the ancients upon being cured gave a cock to Aesculapius, so the nobility, imitating the example of the Prince, began to bestow snuff-boxes of their choosing upon the King of Bath, while those of the middle classes who could afford the token and who craved the distinction soon copied the procedure of their betters.

But the Master was quick to exploit the event of the Prince's visit, to commemorate it in such a way that all—not merely fanciers of snuff-boxes—should become aware of it. He ordered a marble obelisk, thirty feet high, set up in a grove near the Abbey Church. On one side of the pedestal it was to bear the arms of the distinguished patient; and on another, the legend in Latin: 'In memory of the happy restitution of the health of the Prince of Orange, through the favour of God, and to the great joy of Britain, by drinking the Bath waters, 1734'.

Which Princes of the blood, upon hearing of this enduring testimonial, might not next be tempted to try the cure?

A little later an aspiring poetess of the name of Mary Chandler, perhaps not lacking a touch of satire, had some verses printed which she called 'A Description of Bath'. It contained these lines:

> Nor think, O Nash, the Muse forgets thy praise;
> Enough for thee this monument to raise;
> What greater honour can thy pride receive
> Than that thy name with great Nassau shall live?

CHAPTER ELEVEN

ON THE PARADE

IN 1734 the itinerant Abbé Prévost, renowned for his *Memoires d'un homme de qualité*, and even more so for his *Manon Lescaut*, having sought sanctuary in England from religious conflicts which in France he had drawn upon himself, made a tour of the spas. What he had to say of Bath reflected vividly the state of it at the time the Prince of Orange was enjoying its amenities:

'We shall find there', the Abbé noted in *Le pour et le contre*, 'at all times beauties of all ages who come to show off their charms, young girls and widows in quest of husbands, married women who seek solace on account of the unpleasant ones they possess, players making or becoming dupes, musicians, dancers, actors growing rich on the pleasure for which others pay, and sharing it with them; finally, dealers in all kinds of jewels, delicacies and gallantries, taking advantage of a kind of enchantment which blinds everyone in these realms of enchantment, to sell for their weight in gold trifles one is ashamed of having bought after leaving the place'.

The good Abbé was wisely reporting a general view, as if unacquainted with individuals, with men, for example, like Chesterfield—precisely the sort whom he was likely to encounter. In September the Earl arrived. He had known Bath in the 1720s as young Lord Stanhope, in the days when the Countess of Walsingham was being fêted there. Now married to that same Countess, he had returned to Bath for the first time since relinquishing his four-year ambassadorship at the Hague. A peal of twenty-four bells welcomed him, this little undersized man with a big head and a short neck, not much taller than that Prince of Orange whose marriage, incidentally, to the Princess Royal, the Earl played no small part in arranging. It was as well that Chesterfield and the Prince, a dwarfish pair and no mistake, were not in Bath at once, to make, in the presence of Pope, a troupe.

The rubicund Nash, in his white beaver, called as the mummers were serenading Chesterfield at his house in Pierrepoint Street. There was plenty of company: Pope had Martha Blount with him; Lady Suffolk (formerly Henrietta Howard and now a widow), Lady Burlington and Charles Stanhope (cousins to Chesterfield), Bolingbroke, and Lord Herbert's sparkish young brother Robert, called 'Amoretto'.

It was fortunate that they could entertain one another. Not all of the amusements at Bath, try as the Master would, were equally diverting. On a night in October the Earl attended the theatre. Of this experience he noted: 'The Countess of Burlington bespoke the play . . . the audience consisted of seventeen souls'. Drama in Bath was languishing, except the unrehearsed kind out of doors.

After Lady Suffolk had left Bath, Chesterfield (30 October) had this to impart to her: 'Nash (in honour of the King's birthday) gave a ball at Lindsey's . . . he wore his gold-laced clothes on the occasion, and looked so fine that, standing by chance in the middle of the dancers, he was taken by many at a distance for a gilt garland. He concluded the evening, as usual, with basset and blasphemy'. To the Earl, Nash later complained in the same manner of his losses at the tables:

'Would you think it, my lord, that damned bitch Fortune, no earlier than last night, tricked me out of five hundred? Is it not surprising that my luck should never turn, that I should thus eternally be mauled?'

'I don't wonder', returned Chesterfield, 'at your losing money, Nash; but all the world is surprised where you get it to lose'.

The late ambassador, however, had not visited Bath

continuously enough to perceive that where the Master lost once he won five times, through his superior skill at reckoning chances. Nor did Chesterfield yet know that Nash was fond of talking 'poverty' even when he was well ahead of the game.

This festive season suffered something of a loss, at the turn of the year, January 1735, in the death of Thomas Harrison. He had 'lived to enjoy a good estate' from his Assembly-room, and across the way, in Thayer's, his colleague Mrs Lindsey was alert to seize the advantage of the vacancy. She persuaded Nash to let her sister Elizabeth Hayes, a gambler, lease the rooms. While the Master, in the case of Fanny Braddock and other episodes, had experienced his troubles with Mrs Lindsey, he had to grant that 'Lindsey's Rooms' had been profitably run, and he reasoned that the two sisters could work in a harmony which another management in Harrison's might not ensure.

Coincident with the joint beginning of these sisters in Bath occurred the unexpected end of Bell Causey in Tunbridge. She was hardly cold in her coffin before Nash had driven down, and with little ado, on the part of the Town government, got himself installed as Master of Ceremonies. Local keepers of lodgings were delighted if Nash prolonged any visit beyond the mere 'opening of the season', for, like greengrocers in the week before Easter, they arbitrarily raised all their prices, and kept them pegged up, as long as the Beau remained at the spa. In this year, 1735, Nash regulated the Pump-room at Tunbridge to conform with practice at Bath. He decreed likewise that a peal of bells should welcome all fresh arrivals. He engaged competent orchestras. He promulgated rules for the ball-rooms. And he rested on the spot until he saw that these stabilising innovations were well launched.

If life at the Wells was in many ways a duplicate of that at Bath, it did in some particulars differ, with the result that many guests patronised both places in the same year. Society found its focus on the Pantiles. Bands there played twice during the day, and again in the evening except on Tuesday and Friday, when the musicians went into the ball-room. The bookseller's shop existed notably for those who wrote or read verse: budding poets left their lines, usually to a lady or to all of the ladies, to be copied into a large album, for the perusal of whoever wished to read. No written criticism of this poetry was accepted by the bookseller; but oral comment upon it up and down the Pantiles was a pastime of the hour. Away from the centre of things, the amusements included cricket, horse-racing, riding, 'airing in carriages', and excursions to country-houses nearby.

But the Beau as an absentee Master soon ran into difficulties in raising subscriptions either for charity or for entertainments. Visitors to Tunbridge had capitulated to the amiable daily nagging of Bell Causey; but Nash was seldom there long enough at a time to amass sums comparable to hers. He must appoint a deputy, a person known to himself. Upon an early return from Bath he brought with him one Sarah Porter, a woman 'of a certain age', with an unflinching eye, set mouth, and methodical ways. Not at the chapel-door, but at the door of the ball-room, Nash put her on guard, equipped with a folio-book, pen and ink. In no time Mrs Porter, relentless but unruffled, was collecting the dues as thoroughly as Mrs Causey had ever done, and the guests began to call her 'Queen of the Touters'. Unlike her predecessor, however, Sarah Porter appears not to have conducted the gaming-room.

In supervision of all these arrangements at Tunbridge the Master left nothing undone; but contrary to the case in Bath he did not encourage at the Wells much building. Tunbridge had no Ralph Allen, no John Wood. Bath must be emphatically the capital of spas. In this season Wood completed his great work, Queen Square, with its Corinthian façades, upon which he had been engaged for seven years. Nor did the tireless architect rest there.

Straightway he began to fashion Kingsmead Square in the image of the larger plaza.

If the Beau himself was no designer of buildings, he enjoyed some recognition as a landscape-architect, and if not so much in Bath, at least for the estates of so great a lady as the elder Duchess of Marlborough. Having recommended for Blenheim, not long after the Duke died, a great cascade a hundred feet broad as an outlet for its lake, Nash had seen his plan so successfully carried out that the Duchess continued to confer with him as a kind of non-resident steward. In this year the Master was still advising her upon outdoor staff for her various properties. The Duchess was fourteen years older than her favourite. But the formality of their long correspondence only concealed the informality engendered by their friendship. It was a 'practical' association. Everyone in Bath knew the Master of Ceremonies and the Mistress of Blenheim were friends. Nash thereby gained prestige, while the Duchess gained advice from which she benefited.

At the other end of the scale of Nash's ladies continued his mistress, Fanny Murray, the musician's ravishing daughter. She was now at the height of both her attractiveness and her notoriety. Together with the actress Kitty Fisher she had her portrait done. It was described as 'two female figures, beautifully painted, in all their native naked charms'. Those who censured the Master for what they called his 'private life' were bound to grant that he chose his consort with some reason, also that he stood devoted to her alone. He talked much in Bath of 'decorum'. Wherein lay his personal sense of it? He would have replied that he avoided philandering.

Perhaps at the age of sixty-one he could hardly do otherwise. Yet Richard Nash was a pretty fit man for his years. He retained his good Dr Cheyne, but continually jested with him rather than obeyed his orders. One day the Beau called Cheyne in to attend to a minor malady. The doctor wrote out a prescription. Looking in on the next day, Cheyne found his patient up and about.

'Did you follow my prescription?' asked the doctor.

'No', confessed Nash. 'If I had, I should have broken my neck. I flung it out of the two-pair-of-stairs window'.

Yet the Beau was not the only one who raised laughs at the expense of the fat physician; Cheyne, a character almost as distinctive at the waters as Nash himself, was also the butt of anonymous fun-makers. In 1737 the versifier of 'Diseases of Bath', was moved to write thus of the Doctor:

> Big blust'ring Cheyne, not the last in fame,
> Though the Muse lead up in the rear his name,
> Has sent such colonies to Pluto's land,
> The god was forced to beg he'd stop his hand.

Rather than call Cheyne in, this bard preferred that 'Lindsey be my nurse'.

In any such capacity, the manageress of Thayer's rooms could not have long attended him. Sorely in need of nurses herself, she died in August.

The Monarch of Bath could hardly grieve over the loss of this adventuress. For twenty months the two unscrupulous sisters, Mrs Lindsey and Mrs Hayes, had operated the two houses of Assembly to their own enrichment, whilst witholding from the Master his due. In allowing both houses to be controlled by the same family he had yielded to a monopoly impregnable to his own control. Nor was it apparent when Lindsey's maid, Catherine Lovelace, succeeded her, that the new appointment lacked the connivance of Mrs Hayes. Nash sagaciously ruled that the tenure of Lovelace was for the interim only.

Such irregularities in the running of the Assembly-rooms did not preoccupy the Beau unduly. He always had brewing a larger question to engage his exertions. In June 1737 playhouses were suppressed, as well they might be if as Chesterfield noted they drew audiences of only seventeen people. The act of suppression, as it happened, gave to the trustees of the General Hospital the opportunity they had sought for twenty years. They had combed

Bath for a site near enough to the springs on which to build their hospital, their monumental charity. All of the plots they had tried to buy proved far too costly. And now a piece of land both reasonable and suitable came suddenly into the market, at the corner of Union Street and Upper Borough Walls. It was the site of the 'play-room' in which the theatrical performances of Bath had been so precariously staged. The trustees, with such funds as they either had in hand or were promised, bought the property. And they now elected the Beau their joint-treasurer. If Nash's flamboyant collecting of subscriptions had languished from lack of tangible evidence that the hospital was to come into being, this forward step in the scheme gave a fillip to his renewed appeals.

When the Master, no doubt elated by this progress in his long-cherished benefaction, went down to Tunbridge to open the season, he might have read in the album at the bookseller's a few verses to himself, written by a young lady as to a father-confessor:

>Kind caution dwells upon his tongue
> With a paternal care;
>He grieves to see the dangers run
> By each unthinking fair.
>
>Oh, Nash! I fear he strives in vain
> Those evils to prevent;
>Women from vice could ne'er refrain
> When once their minds were bent.
>
>Forgive me on the female cause
> To judgement more refine;
>To yield his merits just applause
> I consciously resign.
>
>Thus Chloe raised her drooping head,
> And sighing, bid adieu.
>Your quick return, dear Nash, she said,
> Hid all my joys in view.

This effort rather sounds as if in 1737 the Beau made two journeys to Tunbridge with only a short interval between them. Whatever his movements were, he did not long interrupt the young lady's flirtations, for the autumnal visit of Chesterfield to Bath was imminent, and Nash seldom absented himself during a visit of that prince of wit.

With his tall German wife, Melusina, the stunted Earl was in Bath for six weeks. After a week of it, although he confided to Lady Suffolk in November that he had recovered from his dyspepsia, headache, and low spirits, he looked upon the rest of his stay as a sort of eternity. He tarried at the Cross Bath, which lately the poetress Mary Chandler had also described:

> Not far from hence, a bath of gentle heat
> The tender virgin finds a safe retreat,
> From sights indecent, and from speeches lewd,
> Which dare not there, with satyr-face, intrude.

But Chesterfield found that the Cross Bath might yet subject a visiting lady to other dangers. A Mrs Buckley thought she was 'in perfect security' until the rather globular Duchess of Norfolk floundered in 'like the great leviathan'. The Duchess raised the waters so high that Mrs Buckley's guide had to carry the little lady about to save her from drowning.

The Earl sauntered round, idled in the Assembly-rooms, but soon wearied 'of playing at low play, which I hate, for the sake of avoiding high play, which I love'. His relatively thrifty though opulent wife would have to make good his losses, and Melusina 'did not like doing dat all de time'.

In this same month, November 1737, the *London Magazine* depicted the scene at Nash's gaming-tables: 'Cards are the universal mode. This diversion might not improperly be called the strategy of shallow people who could not converse, to bring down to a level with themselves those who could . . . for that, gentlemen forgo their distinction of birth and education, waste a whole life in the most trifling of amusements, and bury the noblest faculties in the meanest of employments . . . for this, the ladies pass anxious days and sleepless nights, deny themselves the benefits of light and air, and sacrifice even beauty ... He (the writer) wouldn't have tried to "instruct his betters" if he could have found one day in seven without play. But when on Sunday I went to the public rooms for ... tea, and the pleasure of looking about me, and beheld tables with cards, and surrounded by persons of figure enough to give a sanction to the practice amongst the vulgar, I lost all patience, and could not forbear crying out against a scene so shocking in a Protestant Christian kingdom'.

Yet to Chesterfield, it was shocking only from fear that he might lose high stakes, or from boredom over winning low ones. Thankful though he was, at forty-three, for regaining some of his health impaired in the swirl of London, the only thing in Bath that really diverted him, as he protested to Lady Suffolk, was the gossip—what the duchesses and Mr Herbert were doing. At every scene the Earl put in appearance; he gave every scene its chance. He visited the ball-room, watched the gentlemen 'strut before a wanton ambling nymph'. Said Chesterfield, 'They looked as if they were hired to do it, and were doubtful of being paid'.

Only from his fencing-partner of wit, Beau Nash, could he expect to hear a remark that exhilarated him. The Master, one night, was standing near a fashionable dame who he perceived was sneering.

'I should be pleased', said Nash to her, 'to have your assurance that it is your face you present to mankind'.

CHAPTER TWELVE

THE PRINCE OF WALES

IN 1738 Ralph Allen, who had been quietly gleaning wealth from his regulation and extension of the posts to and from the west of England, and who believed he could gain another fortune if he demonstrated that the stone from the quarry he owned was fit for building on a big scale, commissioned John Wood to build on Coombe Down a house of heroic proportions, to be known as Prior Park. It was to stand 100 feet below the summit of the Down, but 400 feet above Bath. While the 'line' of Prior Park, what with its colonnades outcurving from the central mansion, and beyond them, two cubical houses to mark the extremities, measured about 1,200 feet, the mansion proper, rising to four storeys from a breadth of 100 feet, dominated the whole. Here Wood followed his usual Corinthian style, which he had also used in Allen's earlier house in Lilliput Alley.

It would have pleased Beau Nash, no doubt, to have a hand in the landscape, as he had to his credit done at Blenheim. But the only thing in Bath upon which its triumvirs were acting in concert was the Mineral-Water Hospital. Allen left the gardens of Prior Park to be laid out by Wood and his associates. By way of ornamentation the builders took advantage of a stream, which after crossing the bottom of the lawn facing the house flowed into a lake; at the junction they fashioned a Palladian bridge—like the one in the gardens of Wilton—roofed, to meet a pavilion at either end, set off by columns between, and by flights of steps approaching.

With Wood and Allen thus occupied, Nash shouldered the major responsibility for the Hospital, and in February the trustees sent the Master to London to submit the plans for it to the Royal family. Wood, having designed a plan and elevation of the building, gave his drawings to Nash to take with him. The King approved the plans. Within a week, in the absence of Nash, the trustees opened a subscription to raise the funds already in hand to £6,000, in order to complete demolition of the site, to lay foundations, and to raise the façade. Nash in London promptly turned over his plans to an engraver, then returned home. The success of his mission appeared from the circumstance that by April the trustees had collected more than one-third of the sum required. Workmen straightway began to prepare the ground.

After the actual disappearance of the 'play-room', meagre though the patronage of it had been, visitors began to deplore the lack of a theatre. The Master of Ceremonies was no man to deprive his guests, even a small number of them, of such entertainment as they insisted upon. He therefore dedicated the older Assembly-rooms to performances. A separate theatre also opened in Kingsmead Street in a house, standing some fifteen years, that contained an adaptable room of about twenty-five by fifty feet. The theatre may have been but a halting amusement at Bath; but if the aim of the resort was to please all comers, plays must be provided for the playgoers.

Meanwhile, within about two months after work had started on the Hospital, Nash and his colleagues were ready to lay the foundation-stone. The surroundings were picturesque enough. Along one side stood the famous Bear Inn; a bit farther on ran Lock's Lane, a dark passageway, wherein the houses were so old and overhung that their inhabitants could shake hands from opposite windows. Into this rather congested quarter the intrusion of a spacious new hospital could not have been other than salutary and welcome. The ceremony of the stone-laying, on 6 July, was auspicious. It was announced that Ralph Allen—who was making £16,000 a year out of his postal service—was contributing from his quarry, free of charge, all of the stone needed for the new building. The dignitary chosen to lay the foundation-stone, both a distinguished minister of state and a beneficiary of the waters, was the corpulent William Pulteney. On the legend cut in the stone his name did not appear; but under the date ran the hopeful line, 'God prosper the charitable undertaking'.

The Beau, never flagging, stirred up a good deal of this prosperity himself. Tossing guineas into his white hat, he requested the Duchess of Marlborough to contribute to the hospital as much as he could toss before she compelled him to stop. The Duchess, half playfully, half angrily, tried to howl down Nash's own protestations, but could not make him desist until he had raised the pile to thirty guineas. 'You ugly devil!' she cried. 'I hate the sight of you!' But that evening, at the tables, she was winning, and she allowed him ten guineas more, with her forgiveness.

Nash in this year was said to be 'as great as Alexander at Persepolis'. If a dancing lady touched only the back of an inferior's hand, the Master told her to behave or leave the room. If any couple stopped in the middle of a dance, he told them that unless they finished they would dance no more. If not always ready in wit, he knew the art of saying rude things, on occasion, with such an affable manner that they even pleased. One day in the Grove he joined a party of ladies, of whom one was in figure a bit bent—not an uncommon sight amongst those who took the waters. Nash asked this one whence she came.

'Straight from London', she replied.

'Confound me, madam', said the Master. 'You must have been damnably warped by the way'.

In passing the time of day with such company, he liked to say that as Nestor was a man of three ages, so he,

Nash, was a beau of three generations. 'I have seen flaxen bobs succeeded by majors, which in their turn gave way to negligents, which were at last totally routed by bags and Ramillies'.

Then he recited the manner of *amours* down the generations: 'The lover in the reign of King Charles was solemn, majestic, and formal. He visited his mistress in state, languished for her favour, knelt when he toasted his goddess, walked with solemnity, performed the most trifling things with decorum, and even took snuff with a flourish. The beau of the latter part of Queen Anne's reign was disgusted with so much formality; he was pert, smart, and lively; his *billets-doux* were written in quite a different style from that of his antiquated predecessor; he was ever laughing at his own ridiculous situation, till at last he persuaded the lady to become as ridiculous as himself. The beau of the third age was still more extraordinary than either. His whole secret in intrigue consisted in perfect indifference. The only way to make love now is to take no notice of the lady, which method is the surest way to secure her affection'.

Into the Master's summer of sovereign dalliance now came Chesterfield, in August, not as an infirm gentleman of leisure, but as a leader of the Opposition to Walpole's government. The Earl turned up, Nash very soon found, as harbinger of a royal visitor: Frederick, Prince of Wales. Since the acrimony between the King and his son had hardened beyond the King's endurance, the Opposition naturally turned to the Prince as their standard-bearer, and the men foremost—Chesterfield, Pulteney, Cobham, Pitt, Lyttelton, even Bubb Dodington—had invited him to Bath as part of a political holiday of their own. The reason given out for Frederick's coming, however, was to celebrate the birth of his heir, Prince George, in June last past. The veiled political side of the occasion, of course, was of no concern to the Beau. He was sensible only that Frederick was the biggest 'catch' of the Nash regime. The Master of Ceremonies at once set about collaborating with Chesterfield to put Bath in readiness for the event.

The Prince and Princess, driving down from their house in Maidenhead, arrived at the city gates on 17 October. The Mayor and Corporation met them. After an 'elegant' speech by the Recorder, Frederick made 'gracious' reply. All the Corporation, bareheaded, then walked before the visitors through the principal streets of Bath, until the procession reached the lodgings of the Prince and Princess in Queen Square. Within the lodgings the company, including the Master of Ceremonies, kissed hands.

Frederick was now thirty-one, blonde like his Teutonic mother, but with a good-humoured look, a nose that arched, a dimple in his chin, and eyes almost bovine. Unlike George I and George II, he loved Italian painting and French poetry, also intelligent discussion. The Opposition, finding him neither charmless nor witless, were schooling the Prince to be their leader, even whilst he took his violoncello between his thin legs and played German melodies to those very unmusical lords. All this was known to Beau Nash, to whom Frederick was a spirit more akin.

In the evening the Prince and Princess attended a ball—the official start of the entertainments arranged. Bath was *en fête*. To discipline the tradesmen, its magistrates had regulated food prices. Frederick, not averse to winning popularity, cleared the prison of debtors. In consequence of Nash's visit to London on behalf of the Mineral-Water Hospital, the Prince came prepared to donate to that charity: his gift, no doubt through the good offices of the Beau, was £1,000. It was partly out of gratitude, for he was at the moment benefiting from the waters himself. The celebrations had their paradox: the town presented the Prince with an address on the estranged King's birthday. But Frederick was assured that his visit gave the populace 'all possible happiness' and 'exceeding great joy'.

The gift of the Prince to Bath was a silver cup, cover, and salver. It was a present advisedly made by an heir to a throne. He well knew that in years to come, at feasts of the Corporation, his health, and that of his consort, would in recollection of their sojourn be drunk from this cup. Again, he rewarded the assiduous attentions of Nash by following the vogue: the Prince added to the Master's collection of snuff-boxes, presenting one that was larger than those usually given him, and gold-enamelled.

Early in November the royal visitors, having served their purpose both social and political, brought all this jubilation to a close, and departed. Bath had in Nash's time seen no festivities of comparable dimensions. If the response of the Master of Ceremonies to a snuff-box from the Prince of Orange had been an obelisk thirty feet high, his acknowledgement of a larger snuff-box from the Prince of Wales must surely be nothing less than an obelisk sixty feet high. Nash so ordered the monument, to be set up in Queen Square, and to face the very lodgings distinguished by Frederick. Of this obelisk, in its measurements, there was an historic prototype: the needle dedicated at Heliopolis to Rameses, in the time of the Trojan War.

The question of a proper inscription remained. Nothing would satisfy Nash but some euphonious lines from the hand of the first poet of the age, Alexander Pope. The Master reckoned that he could with confidence appeal to Pope, who was now not only an annual patient at the waters, but who professed affection for Nash himself. His own pen, the Beau always said, was 'a torpedo in his hand'. He now wrote to the poet that no words (meaning no words by Nash) could express the gratitude he felt for the favour of the Prince. But the Master of Ceremonies was sure that Pope could put into writing those feelings of Nash on a theme so moving.

Pope in reply demurred, with a touch of his mock modesty and more than a touch of his prevarication. 'I am the worst person you could have pitched upon for this purpose, who have received so few favours from the great myself, that I am utterly unacquainted with what kinds of thanks they like best. Whether the Prince most loves poetry or prose, I protest I do not know'. He ended by affirming that Nash could give Frederick as much satisfaction in either as Pope could, and signed himself Nash's 'affectionate servant'.

For all his genius in observing character, Pope had evidently not gauged in Nash his quality of perseverance. The Beau only renewed his appeal. After some lapse of time, Pope answered, excusing his delay on the plausible grounds that he had tried first to find a writer 'properer' than himself, then to enquire of the Prince's friends what sort of inscription might be acceptable. In the end the poet had compromised by way of plain words, 'nearly the common sense of the thing', upon which he 'did not know how to flourish'. (The mere use of that one word, 'flourish', betrayed Pope's supreme ability if he had chosen to exercise it.) But he was offhand, bored with the whole task. 'This you would do as well', he assured Nash in conclusion, 'or better, yourself, and I dare say may mend the expression'. So little did Pope care that he would permit the unpoetic Beau to tamper with the lines. The postscript was characteristic: 'I think I need not tell you my name should not be mentioned'.

Pope's inscription, to be cut in nine lines, read simply, 'In memory of honours bestowed, and in gratitude for benefits conferred, in this city, by His Royal Higness, Frederick, Prince of Wales, and his Royal Consort, in the year 1738, this obelisk is erected by Richard Nash, Esq'.

Immemorially a harried author, confronted by an admirer with a copy of the author's book to inscribe, has sat down for a few anguished moments—whilst the admirer waits in blissful anticipation—and at length turned out the witty phrase, 'Yours truly'.

The Beau, no critic of literature whatever else he might be, accepted 'the common sense of the thing', and ordered Pope's words engraved. It was in the setting of the obelisk that Nash slaked his own thirst for expression. He enclosed the monument with a stone balustrade, which he embellished, in the middle of each side, by iron gates regally wrought.

With the backing of the Corporation the Master found it no hardship to collect the cost of this marble souvenir—eighty pounds.

CHAPTER THIRTEEN

EO

A CERTAIN house in Bath, built not by John Wood but by an inferior and rather quixotic architect, was said to be haunted. No mere ghostly creature roamed within it; the offending spirit was a devil. The house looked like a bandbox surmounted by a kind of Tom Tower, bore ornamental pots round its roof, and contained a door with an Ionic portico. Workmen said the house frightened passing horses. While Nash was not too concerned about the tranquillity of the horses, he wanted to let it be known that in his capacity as guardian of the peace he was at all times better than indifferent. He sought out the rector of St. Michael's, whom he begged to drive the devil from Bath, 'if only to please the ladies'.

Whatever steps the rector may have taken, the question of the devil in Bath was in the view of some persons a thing that reached beyond the walls of a bandbox house. In April 1739, John Wesley and his brother Charles, in the flush of their eloquence at thirty-six and thirty-two, appeared amongst the visitors, with the set purpose of making the town uncomfortable for Satan. John Wesley was fresh-faced, with his hair combed smooth except at the ends, which he curled a bit. He could speak a sermon so fast that it sounded 'like a lesson'. Charles, as the militant seconder of John, if not so dynamic on the rostrum, could in any situation turn a pungent phrase impromptu.

Called with their followers in Oxford 'methodists',

from the strictness of their devotions, the Wesleys had proceeded to the new American colony of Georgia (Charles as secretary to its governor and John to conduct a mission), returned in 1738 to England and declared themselves 'converted', and had lately opened a Methodist chapel in Bristol. From Bristol they were now making religious forays into the countryside.

In Bath, on 23 April, John Wesley delivered his first exhortation, to a crowd whose numbers gave him more satisfaction than surprise. Reflecting in his journal upon this meeting, he observed: 'There was great expectation at Bath, of what a noted man (Nash) was to do to me there, and I was much entreated not to preach, because no one knew what might happen. By this report I gained a much larger audience, among whom were many of the rich and great'. However, the audience, some 4,000 poeple, were rather disappointed, inasmuch as their 'noted' man was not one of them. And Wesley, like a border-raider, withdrew to Bristol.

When a month later he turned up a second time he preached to only a quarter of his original congregation, again without being honoured by the attendance of the Beau. Nevertheless Wesley spoke with such fervour, and at the end of his sermon acted with such 'vulgar enthusiasm', that he threw a housemaid into convulsions. This might have been regarded nothing more than an incident; but the fit kept the girl writhing for fourteen hours. Her master turned her away, because 'he would have none in his house who had received the Holy Ghost'. The comment of Charles Wesley was, 'Satan took it ill to be attacked in his headquarters'.

This was too much for the Master of Ceremonies. A week thereafter, 5 June, when John Wesley undertook to preach a third time, at the hour of breakfast, Nash had his band, augmented by three French horns and three kettle-drums, play against the evangelist. And this time the Beau himself, 'their champion', as Wesley dubbed him, appeared, at a moment when 'many of them were sinking into seriousness'; and Nash stood close to the disturber.

'By what authority', the Master demanded, 'are you preaching at Bath?'

'By that of Jesus Christ', returned Wesley with spirit, 'conveyed to me by the present Archbishop of Canterbury, when he laid his hands upon me and said, "Take thou authority to preach the gospel!"'

'You are acting contrary to the laws', persisted Nash. 'Besides, your preaching frightens people out of their wits'.

'Sir, did you ever hear me preach?'

'No'.

'How then can you judge of what you never heard?'

'By common report'.

'Sir, is not your name Nash? I dare not judge of you by common report'.

The Beau was not at a loss to shift his ground. 'What do the people come here for?' he enquired.

Before even Wesley could retort a female voice in the crowd cried out: 'Let an old woman answer him. You, Mr Nash, take care of your body: we take care of our souls, and for the good of our souls we come here'.

The Monarch of Bath knew when his throne was shaken. He withdrew, and to a considerable distance. The summer was more agreeable at Tunbridge Wells, where, to the young ladies who sang his praises in verse, *he* was father-confessor. Still more to the point, the Prince and Princess of Wales, as if to reinforce their patronage of the Master of Ceremonies, after so happy a visit to Bath, were now sojourning at the Wells. To Nash's mind, more divinity hedged Frederick than Wesley. And only a furlong from the Pantiles, the Beau might capture new vigour, even at sixty-five, in the cold bath.

To return home for the autumn season in Bath was to find a pert young miss of nineteen, Elizabeth Robinson, one of the centres of admiration. While her dark hair, blue eyes, and faultless complexion were hardly enough to engage unusual notice, her vitality was such that she could write letters or read all day, and dance the night through. It was her independence of spirit, her gibing at casual acquaintance, that accounted for her attractiveness. Already she had visited the races and assemblies for years, during which time she met the young Duchess of Portland, six years older, a girl who at twenty had married the Duke, and who now called Elizabeth her 'dear Fidget'.

The scene to which Nash came back Miss Robinson thus described to the Duchess: 'The morning after I arrived I went to the Ladies' Coffee-House, where I heard of nothing but the rheumatism in the shoulder, the sciatica in the leg, and the gout in the toe. After these complaints I began to fancy myself in the hospitals or infirmaries; I never saw such an assembly of disorders. I daresay Gay wrote his "Court of Death" from this place. After drinking the waters I go to breakfast, and about twelve I drink another glass of water; visits employ the afternoon, and we saunter away the evening in great stupidity. I think no place can be less agreeable. "How d'ye do?" is all one hears in the morning, and "What's trumps?" in the afternoon'.

Grumbling in Bath constituted part of its cure, if not part of its charm. Miss Robinson might suffer the radiance of the great. Chesterfield came in October, Pope in November. Pope of course grumbled loudest of all. 'But for your news of me quitting Twik'nam for Bath', he confided to Samuel Richardson at this time, 'enquire into my years, if they are past the bounds of dotage. Ask my eyes, if they can see, and my nostrils, if they can smell. To prefer rocks and dirt to flowery meads and silver Thames, and brimstone and fogs to roses and sunshine. When I arrive at these sensations, I may settle at Bath, of which I never yet dreamt, further than to live just out of the sulphurous pit, and at the edge of the fogs at Mr Allen's for a month or so. I like the place so little, that health itself should not draw me thither, though friendship has twice or thrice'. Unlike Miss Robinson, the great little man had the excuse of age. He was now fifty-one, and no longer relished the gaieties of Bath as he had done when at half his years.

If Pope and Elizabeth Robinson, Chesterfield and the rest, were the figures of mark in whom Nash found his daily zest, he was too able a ruler to devote to them overmuch time. Greatly sympathetic, he kept an eye upon the distressed in his community. The oncoming winter of 1739 threatened to be peculiarly hard upon people of small means, and the Master, knowing that many of them were 'too proud to beg', went into their houses, enquiring into their necessities, and either sent gifts in kind or left donations in cash. Colliers were out of work. They loaded a wagon with coals, themselves drew it into Bath, and presented it to Nash. He undertook a subscription for them, starting it with ten guineas of his own. Weavers were going hungry. When they came begging into Bath, the Beau set up for them a great feast, and when the men went away, he gave to each a week's subsistence.

His response to this kind of begging elevated the hopes of beggars who did nothing else. Bath and its suburbs were tormented with them. Often in bogus rags, often exhibiting bogus ailments, they roamed the streets, pretending to live there for the waters, preying upon visitors. Nash, even whilst he was helping the poor in other directions, was not to be any longer imposed upon by the pseudo-poor. He persuaded the Corporation in this same year, 1739, to pass an Act to suppress beggars, those who 'infested the streets in their rags and diseases', by the chastening expedient of committing them to the House of Correction for a year at hard labour. After a generation of experience, the Master was more than capable of discriminating between one beggar and another.

His generosity to the weavers and colliers, however, came none too soon, for the same season impaired his income by bringing into effect a law against gambling. It prohibited such games as faro, basset, hazard, and ace of hearts, under penalty of £200, one-third of which was to go to the informer, and the rest to the new hospital. If the gambler who was apprehended did not possess this fine, his goods were forfeit. The award to the hospital, Nash's pet scheme, was ironic. Much as the Beau might approve such an allocation of the penalties, he foresaw in this statute against gaming, unless it could be got round, an end to his personal charities.

The 'getting round' was not long in coming, by the simple device of inventing a new game, called passage. It caught as many players as the old ones, impoverishing the majority, enriching the few. Again the law intervened, in 1740, to decree that any game at all, 'with numbers thereon', should bear, for inventor and player alike, the same penalty as the other games outlawed. Once more the players exercised their inventive talents, devising, within the law, one new game called rolly-polly, and another known as Marlborough's battles. At this point Walter Wiltshire took over from Catherine Lovelace the management of Thayer's (Lindsey's) rooms.

In the thick of this realignment of the gaming, Nash changed mistresses. Such a shift he could endure without wincing. If his mistress approved him, good; if not, let her go. And the time came when Fanny Murray went. There was no breaking of Nash's heart for love. 'Women', said he, 'are as plentiful as mushrooms, always to be had for the asking'. He was a theorist on questions of sentiment. 'Good humour and fine clothes', the Master once said, 'are enough to debauch a nunnery; but the art of saying nothing is worth both. Always talk to women in the language they understand. As soon as you speak rationally, the game is up. Learned men, therefore, make indifferent lovers'.

The lady whom he chose to succeed Fanny revelled in the name of Juliana Papjoy. She was said to be a dressmaker, who also went a-simpling, that is, engaged in the guileless summer occupation of picking herbs. A rhymester, long afterward, referred to Juliana as the 'Bishopstrowe belle', a dark and haughty young woman who spurned all admirers until one day Nash appeared at her house, and subsequently lured her from Wiltshire to Bath. At all events she now went to live with the Master in St. John's Court. He provided her with a dapple-grey riding-horse, and with a whip of many thongs. Whereupon Juliana left off making dresses, except for herself, and proceeded to ride about the streets of Bath. In no time her singular whip had earned her the title of 'Lady Betty Besom'.

Whether she was in evidence in St. John's Court—Nash's house was now called the Garrick's Head—on the next visit of royalty to Bath is an arresting question. Early in the season of 1740 Princess Mary, fourth daughter of George II and wife of the Landgrave of Hesse, was due to arrive with her niece, Princess Caroline. Since the visit of the Prince of Wales the fame of the gracious hospitality of the Beau had spread far amongst the reigning family. Nash rode forth to meet the two princesses at Sandy Lane, and to pay his compliments to the elder. After the usual flourish of trumpets, his cavalcade escorted the royal guests into Hetling House, a part of the Westgate Buildings.

The reception, thus far, was quite in keeping with the finished performance of which the Master was capable. On the next day he with equal charm accompanied the princesses to the places of assembly. As they were making their rounds, a fire unaccountably broke out in Hetling House, and although enough persons chanced to be in the neighbourhood at the time to lend a hand to put out the fire, the Princesses were unable to occupy the house for the night approaching. Nash invited them to the Garrick's Head, and there they slept. So did Juliana Papjoy. But the Princess Mary was pleased, for on departing from Bath she left ten guineas for those who had quenched the fire at Hetling House.

Not Bath ablaze, but Bath in the process of building was the thing to behold whenever royal guests appeared. New buildings, which the town seemed ever to be adding, both quickened their interest and invited their patronage. The new hospital, under the combined energy of Nash, Dr William Oliver (who in this year became physician to the hospital), Ralph Allen and John Wood, was going forward apace, on the strength of a fund at present amounting to £4,268. Again, in March, the tireless Wood laid the first stone of the North Parade. His idea was to make the structure look like one house, and therefore like a palace. The façade was to include the laying out of a promenade—for the ladies in their wide hoops and high head-dress, for pert abigails, frisky lap-dogs, ladies attended by a powdered beau babbling rhymes or the newest scandal. Such a cast of characters Wood foresaw, on a promenade leading to the bowling-green; to hear the band, to walk along the river-bank, and bring up at Spring Gardens.

Although on the building-sites all continued to go smoothly for the Master of Ceremonies, he could not feel so serene about his position at the gaming-tables. The restrictive laws in respect of 'numbers' hindered him. But on one of his periodic visits to Tunbridge he found the assembly playing a new game which sidestepped the law merely by substituting letters for numbers. It was called E O, for even and odd. Invented by one Cook, this game was highly profitable to the bank, since it took two and a half per cent on all that was either lost or won. Cook and the manager of the assembly divided these profits, and in addition, E O afforded its owners an advantage of five per cent.

Nash studied this table of play. The game was a kind of simplified roulette. The E O table was circular, about four feet across, and with the letters E and O marked round the rim. Within the rim revolved a shallow cone in which a ball rolled, while at the rim, in forty niches, E's and O's alternated, into one of which, at the end of the spin, the ball lodged. The owners reserved two 'bar' niches out of the forty; if into either one the ball fell, the owners won all the bets upon the letter opposite that niche, nor did they pay to the niche into which the ball fell.

No sooner had the Beau discerned the possibilities in this game for relieving his own straits than the Tunbridge manager, covetous of all the profits, turned the inventor Cook out of the assembly-room. But Cook was no man to suffer defeat humbly. At once he hired a crier to warn everyone away from E O as played in that room. Whereupon the manager came running to Nash, to whom he offered a quarter of the bank if he would drive the crier off the Pantiles. The Beau needed money, if for nothing more than for his charities at Bath. He accepted.

Still Cook was not to be downed. On the day thereafter, he got hold of Nash as readily as the manager had done, and tried to bribe Nash out of his bargain. The reward was to be a half share—double the offer of the manager, if the Beau would help Cook set up a rival game of E O. But Nash refused to let his manager down.

Cook, resourceful as ever, then went about to secure another backer. Him he found in a man called Joye; and they opened their competing E O. The next development was that Joye and Cook, lacking the prestige and the convenient location of the regular assembly-room at Tunbridge, failed to fill their table of play by half. It was then Joye's turn to seek out Nash, and protest, probably on the ground that the Beau owed something to Cook as the inventor of the game. Rather belatedly Nash recognised this obligation. He persuaded his manager to join banks with Cook and Joye, the two tables to commend patrons to each other. What was in the back of Nash's head, however, was that as negotiator he claimed a third of the profits of the joint concern, while to his manager he allotted a second third, and to Cook and Joye the other third. Thus ended the E O war at Tunbridge.

All this time, of course, the Master was preparing to

introduce so lucrative a game as E O at Bath. He first got assurance from his lawyers that E O was not illegal. As at Tunbridge, he found various noblemen who had voted to suppress gaming were ready to encourage E O. He therefore proposed to the two assembly-rooms that each buy a table, and, following his scheme at Tunbridge, though a bit more liberally, suggested that in return for his sanction, and his protection, they give him a quarter of the profits.

Wiltshire readily agreed, as the phrase goes, in principle. Mrs Hayes, who was still in charge at the assembly now known as Simpson's, was all the more eager. She was just espoused to an impecunious peer, Lord Hawley, upon whom she was bestowing a part of her moderate fortune for his title. However, when the cost of setting up the E O tables was taken into account, Lady Hawley and Wiltshire prevailed upon Nash to reduce his share of the winnings to one-fifth.

From faraway regions of England the gamblers flocked in to the new game, secure in their belief that it was within the law. Bath took on a new life. Whether in Simpson's or in Wiltshire's, by the dim light from candelabra, the rattle of dice, the shuffle of cards, the clink of glasses, the jingle of coin, mingled with the ripple of balls at E O. So commented one writer upon the scene, and added that 'Nash was insouciant'. And why not? He stood in a fair way of aging into a rich old man. A quatrain of doggerel of the time ran in this wise:

> Nash represents man in the mass,
> Made up of wrong and right,
> Sometimes a knave, sometimes an ass
> Now blunt and now polite.

CHAPTER FOURTEEN

THE GREAT HOSPITAL

IN November 1741 Ralph Allen, now alderman of Bath, opened Prior Park. Wood had taken three years to build it, with its hexastyle portico, its pavilions, its great arcades outcurving like open arms, its luxuriant gardens and Palladian bridge—the landmark of Coombe Down. To ride round the grounds, all enclosed, was to ride a distance of fifteen miles, affording on the circuit varying views of Bath, the Avon, and the adjacent country. The gardens abounded in sculpture, also various. At the head of a waterfall stood Moses striking the rock. On the lawn in front of the great house towered a statue of General Wade, Allen's father-in-law and benefactor, in Roman costume, truncheon in hand. And Prior Park as a whole was Allen's retort to the architects of London, who had rejected his Bath-stone as material fit for a house.

Here Allen and his second wife, Elizabeth Holder, a short grey-haired lady of winning countenance, meant to entertain the intellectuals, for although Allen built Prior Park for all Bath to see—from a distance—he did not intend that all should swarm into it. Yet as a host he always bore his affluence with humility, dressing in plain 'Quaker-coloured' garb, and in shirtsleeves with only a chitterlin up the slit. The house itself, indoors as well as out, was nothing Quakerish. It contained a gallery ninety feet long, a promenade of art. At the end of the left wing of the house there was a charming pavilion, wherein Allen designed to take breakfast or tea with his intimates. The dining-room was stately, seating thirty, who were to dine off Dresden.

No celebrity in Bath could set the level of Allen's aims more fitly than Alexander Pope. He was there at this time, and he went up to Prior Park. It is not on record that Beau Nash accompanied him. But as long as Nash and Allen remained closely associated upon a building of equal import to the community, the new hospital, the Master of Ceremonies could be well content to survey Prior Park from afar.

Indeed the opening of this hospital, the prime benefaction of Richard Nash, suddenly became a settled thing. On Christmas Eve the trustees—Nash, Dr Oliver, John Wood and the rest—met to choose a matron and to open an annual subscription to sustain patients who were poor. Not only did they agree at once upon the woman to be selected; each trustee put down a handsome sum for the fund. Immediately after this meeting a lady of means, one Mrs Jane Holden, impressed by the example of the trustees, handed over a Christmas gift of £2,000. It was the kind of windfall that the Beau had awaited for years. He and his colleagues forthwith fixed the date for unlocking the doors of their sanitarium: 18 May.

The hospital had risen upon its site almost concurrently with Prior Park, Wood having finished Allen's house only a few months earlier. Fortuitously the election in 1742 of Allen as Mayor enabled him to appear on the first day at the hospital both as officer and as donor. The building showed three Ionic sides of about ninety feet each, being left open to the south, and these sides consisting of 'a ground, principal, and chamber storey'. Above the main door, flanked by five windows either side, was 'proposed' a bas relief of the Good Samaritan.

Wood distributed the accommodations handily. Off the vestibule he built rooms for the apothecary, the doctors, the matron, and the surgeons, while in the west front he placed a committee-room, a secretary's room, and a steward's room. The west wing also contained a men's ward, as the east housed the women, and above, the 'chamber storey' provided five more wards, to a total of 108 beds. Quarters for the staff took up the ground floor.

Within a month after the opening, Chesterfield arrived for the summer, to join the trustees and to count the contributions, which now extended to a sum of £8,643. 'Your alkaloid mercury', he told Dr Cheyne, 'and your burgundy, have proved my two most constant friends. I find my shattered tenement' (he was only forty-eight) 'admits of but half repairs, and requires them annually'. The Earl was a power on the board of the twenty-three trustees, amongst whom the order of precedence was Ralph Allen as chairman, Chesterfield, Nash, and Dr Oliver—to whom all the rest deferred.

On 23 June they drew up a 'scheme of rules' for the hospital, and when they had done, they counted forty-one of them, all to be read aloud in each ward every Tuesday morning. These rules were as exacting upon the officers and visitors as upon nurses and patients. There was to be no swearing, smoking, nor gambling; and all fit convalescents were to assist in nursing and domestic work. Past experience, perhaps, prompted a special curb upon the matron: she was not to dispose of any old clothes of deceased patients except by direction. Nor was any inhabitant of Bath eligible for admission to the general hospital, since they could enjoy the waters in their own houses.

All this excitement round the hospital somewhat distracted the Beau from his own financial affairs. While he had been thriving upon his one-third of E O from Tunbridge, and upon his one-fifth from Bath, he now grew a little concerned over certain lapses in payment, particularly from Tunbridge. He had trusted his three 'confederates', the manager, Cook, and Joye, and had visited the Wells no oftener than before the days of E O. Absent in Bath, he had neglected to estimate how much his share ought to be. Nor had he ever enquired of Tunbridge how much in a given period was won and lost, since Cook and the others lulled him by a fair beginning, and had at stated intervals transmitted likely sums. But suddenly Nash found reason to believe that this trio had cheated him out of 2,000 guineas. Whereupon he proceeded against his manager, who had eluded even the vigilance of such a woman as Sarah Porter.

In Bath, naturally, the Master was able to observe Wiltshire and Lady Hawley more closely; yet they took advantage of his absorption in a multiplicity of details away from the Assembly-rooms, and their manipulations of the bank were not easy to penetrate. All that Nash could be sure of was that his own receipts were shrinking. When he complained, Wiltshire and Lady Hawley each offered the Beau £100 a year to relinquish his share of the profits. This he refused. He contented himself for the moment with the thought that these managers now knew they were being watched.

If the Master at present had less money for himself, he delighted in getting more for the hospital. Nash was blessed with a happy faculty of feeling opulent as long as funds were passing through his hands, whether the sums were for his own use or not. In October he started yet another subscription for that hospital, the building famous almost a generation before it took shape. The King himself, by way of Nash, contributed £200. The Prince of Wales sent £50 more, and so did his Princess. Contributions tailed off with gifts from such dignitaries as the Bishop of Worcester, and the Beau, Bathonian Monarch for all his clipped income, put in £100 of his own. Few collectors for charity had collected so often from themselves.

Efforts of this kind drew their praises. The force of Nash's leadership continued to be acknowledged, and only a few months later, in February 1743, the *Gentleman's Magazine* printed some verses from one writing 'at Bath, where great Nash his genius shows'. The author called his lines 'The Hat of Honour, or King of Bath':

> Beaux, belles and bishops—nay, the judge and wit
> To his decision nod, at once submit;
> Both court and country partizans unite,
> And every season deem their Dick the Knight.
> Not the red ribbon more respect can claim,
> Than the White Hat of everlasting fame
> At balls, the pump, parade, or at the play,
> Each sex, all ages, ready homage pay;
> A bow, a smile, a whisper, or a hand,
> By turns employed, does every heart command.
> O! would that ruby face forever shine,
> The fair, as now, might still appear divine.

One does not hear the name of the Beau echoing down the centuries as 'Dick' Nash. Yet in 1743, even at the age of sixty-nine, he seems on occasion to have been so called. Not from every direction, however, did 'ready homage' come, for in this same year Dr John Burton, a classical scholar so tall that he was called 'the Giant', being in Bath, rather 'looked down' upon its Master of Ceremonies: 'a silly overlord, a worn-out and toothless old man, crowned with a white hat, and whose face was animated iron-rust, changeless and shameless red'.

To 'Giant Jack', the local luminary who merited better words was Ralph Allen, the lord of Prior Park: 'a man worth a thousand, whose presence amongst them the walls everywhere proclaim; whom the want of high birth renders the more illustrious, and shows him to be at once the child of virtue and the favourite of fortune, self-formed, self-taught, and self-complete; a man whom one may call, if not the most learned, yet certainly, upon comparison with most, a man of letters, and one who by his literary commerce (the posts) has deservedly acquired an ample and unenvied fortune'. Evidently Burton had been more agreeably received at Prior Park than in the Pump-room.

If Burton did call at the great house on Coombe Down he found worshipful society—Pope, Bolingbroke, Chesterfield, all of whom, in the high summer, were devoting their holiday now to Allen, now to Nash. Pope's doctor had ordered garlic for him. If the man was Cheyne, that prescription was about his last, for the good Falstaffian physician died in this year at seventy-two, a victim of his own obesity. By none of his patients would his loss be felt more keenly than by the Master of Ceremonies, who for all his badinage with Cheyne esteemed him above any other doctor in Bath.

The present infirmity of Nash, however, was less physical than financial. Since his partners in E O both at Tunbridge and at Bath had swindled him—for a total, the Beau reckoned, of £20,000—he decided to sue not only his Tunbridge manager but Walter Wiltshire as well. The suit presently came to nothing, on the ground that the agreement into which Nash had entered with these men was 'immoral'. Nor was that the worst of the case. By going to court, the Master unwisely made public what he had previously with great care concealed: that instead of being merely the benevolent supervisor of the Assembly-rooms, he received a slice of their winnings. The public had taken no exception to gains he visibly won. But now it came to light that the King of Bath was a confederate of the managers, and if the association roused little animosity, his straits brought him equally little sympathy. His major mistake was simply that in neither Tunbridge nor Bath had he appointed anyone to scrutinise the accounts on his behalf.

For all this adversity, the Beau retained both his post and his power. Tuesday night found him at Lady Hawley's assembly (Lord Hawley in this year died), while Friday found him at Wiltshire's, however 'worn out, toothless and rusty' the old leader might be. But he was not so 'silly' as Burton thought. Nash still knew what was brewing in the social background, if not in the financial. One night in Wiltshire's he stepped up to a wealthy lady and her young daughter, and to the mother said firmly:

'Madam, you had better be at home.'

The lady turned away, highly offended, upon which the Master followed her and repeated his advice.

Thinking then that there was something in this more

than impertinence, mother and daughter did retreat to their lodgings. They discovered at the door a coach-and-six. A sharper was on the point of eloping with the elder daughter of the family.

Thus, what Nash lost upon one side of his reputation he regained upon the other, and he might still have remained relatively serene in his eminence had not a deadly tightening of the law against gambling throttled Bath in 1745. By this new enactment, all play, except at cards, was stopped at the end of June. Nor was any 'house, room, or place' to be kept for gambling, upon pain of forfeiture. Any person present at a gaming-table, player or not, might be summoned. Anyone who lost ten pounds at a sitting was liable to indictment within six months thereafter, and on conviction, was to be fined five times the sum won or lost. This was the end of roulette, of E O, of all the games devised to 'get round' the earlier laws.

The immediate effect upon Nash was naturally to send him into a very bad humour. An observer of him about a fortnight later (13 July), after remarking upon the Beau's 'monstrous white hat, motley distinguished garb, and uncouthly affected or broken manner of speech', went on to record: 'He is doubtless of consequence in this place; public diversions would scarcely be so well regulated without his direction. It is to be wished he would take pains to discountenance oaths and profane speeches, as greater blemishes to beaux in a public assembly, than white aprons can be to bellies, though at a ball'. Forty years earlier Nash had ruled against swearing; he was now losing his grip, and so were the gamblers.

Nevertheless the popularity of Bath as a resort seemed hardly to subside. It held its own. Visitors continued to come in fresh relays, if only for cards. This was partly due to the circumstance that Tunbridge Wells was no longer so fashionable. In October Elizabeth Robinson, now Mrs Montagu, the lady with deep-set eyes and the touch of winsome complacency, wrote from the Wells: 'Here are

Hungarians, French, Portuguese, Irish, and Scotch. Also Jews, Catholics, gaunt Puritans and rigid Presbyterians. I never saw a worse collection of human creatures'. The lady was hard to please; but there was truth in what she said. Her friends were putting in more of their time at Bath, largely owing to the havoc wrought at Tunbridge by Nash's former accomplices Cook and Joye.

But there was a wide gap between the condition of Bath and the condition of Beau Nash. With gambling shut down, with gambling-debts not valid in law, with sharpers and fortune-hunters absenting themselves for fear of arrest, and with the nobility withdrawn into their own houses to gamble only with one another, the pickings for the Master grew meagre indeed, and his charities, once so lavish, came to a halt. His personal donations to the hospital alone would have been enough to tide him over present stringency. Nor were enemies slow to rise up round him: anonymous writers accused him of fraudulent dealings. At length the Beau had to quit his sumptuous mansion in St. John's Court, and move into a little house in Saw Close. His one consolation in this new address was that it was almost opposite the old one, and friends of former years who came to look him up in his kingly quarters could hardly lose their way in trailing him to his more modest surroundings.

The shift in his fortunes put Nash rather desperately on the defensive. As the rumours against his integrity increased, he resorted to the flamboyant expedient of having circulars printed, hand-bills, which 'stated his case', and these he pressed upon his acquaintance, both local and visiting, all and sundry, whenever he encountered them. In these apologies the Master did not hesitate to elaborate his private dealings with Wiltshire and Lady Hawley, whose perfidy he exposed. But if these accusations vilified his accomplices, the glaring fact stood forth that Nash himself had been an accomplice of theirs. At seventy he had forgotten the frequent identity of excuse with self-accusation.

CHAPTER FIFTEEN

DECLINE

SO high had been the ascent of the Bathonian Monarch, so firm his power, and so ubiquitous his presence, that he long weathered the ill wind. Most of the visitors never noticed that the helm was slipping from his clutch. The patronage of royalty continued to draw attention to his leadership: early in 1746 came the Princess Caroline, 'for her rheumatism'; in August came the Princess Margaret of Hesse, also to take the waters. Little cared they that in the Assembly-rooms dice no longer rattled, wheels no longer spun. Princess Margaret enlivened the scene for two months, including Coronation Day, 11 October. When for that day Nash announced a ball in celebration, it was at the Assembly more to the point than gambling that the Princess was able by way of overture to contribute a 'drawing-room'.

Chesterfield was of the company. He noted that Nash's white hat still commanded more respect than the crown of some kings. Nash was still talking of the coalition of parties and ranks for Bath, still exacting good manners of dancers, humouring good society, suppressing scandal and late hours—although it was true that his splendour was not as shining as of old. He had recently found it imperative to sell his dazzling collection of snuff-boxes.

If visits of Princesses afforded only a temporary fillip to the curtailed excitement of Bath, a new diversion, the theatre, might oftener relieve the void. In 1747 Nash permitted John Hippisley to build a theatre in Orchard

Street. Hippisley was a comedian of long experience in Lincoln's Inn Fields and Covent Garden, having played Shallow, Dogberry, Fluellen, and 'created' the part of Peachum in Gay's *Beggars' Opera*. In respect of Bath, of course, he was remembered from 1725, for his Captain Whiffle in Odingsells' *Bath Unmasked* at Lincoln's Inn Fields. He now set to work, with £1,000, upon a theatre in Doric style, forty feet front by sixty in depth. Appointing himself as manager, Hippisley had a motto ready for his 'Bath Company of Comedians' before he had a roof on the house:

> Plays are like mirrors made, for men to see
> How bad they are, how good they ought to be.

Nor was this the only innovation to enliven the subdued tone of the resort. The assembly-rooms opened for concert-breakfasts. Each gentleman was entitled to a stated number of tickets for ladies at 1s. 9d. each, and people of 'rank and fortune' who were musically inclined joined with the performers. Modest as the price of the meals was, the subscriptions exceeded the outlay, and after three breakfasts, ending on 1 May 1747, the managers donated a surplus of £28 to the General Hospital.

This hospital was still Nash's prime charity, the monument of his kingship, although by it he had partly impoverished himself. If he could now contribute no more funds, he could support it by his influence. There was one restriction in its management that had always disturbed him: it did not admit the local poor, the people who lived in Bath. In this year Nash was instrumental in opening a house for patients from five parishes: St. Peter and Paul, St. James, St. Michael, Walcot, and Bathwick. It was called the Pauper Charity. This annex rounded out the work of his original benefaction.

On the heels of this opening, the Master was in 1748 accused of embezzling 'some funds raised by public subscription for a charitable purpose'. The charge forced

Nash, for once, to refer to his own philanthropy. Protesting in the *Bath Journal*, he said: 'It has cost me more money annually on the public account, than any ten (people) that ever came to Bath, and if it was not for the sake of Bath and company, I would leave 'em to the chaos I found 'em in'.

While there was to a degree both truth and justice in these words, some of 'the great' who formerly did him homage chose not to hear. Whereupon the old Beau began to seek plaudits from ordinary folk whom in earlier years he would rarely have taken time to notice. But his manner with them, though intended to be witty, was apt to prove unfortunate. He asked one such lady to dance a minuet. She declined. 'Have you got bandy legs?' demanded Nash. If the physical defects of another person were visible, he made fun of them audibly. This style of behaviour began to engender retorts in kind, at which the disconcerted Master grew peevish. He had seldom put up with 'back talk' from the lesser ranks.

It was in a recalcitrant strain of this nature that in the same year, 1748, Tobias Smollett wrote and published *Roderick Random*, in which, depicting a scene in the Long Room at the assembly, he sharply sketched the status of Nash at the time. Roderick, having accompanied his young friend Miss Snapper to the ball, told how the Master tried to expose her 'to the edge of his wit': 'The celebrated Mr Nash . . . approached us, with many bows and grimaces, and, after having welcomed Miss Snapper to the place, asked her, in the hearing of all present, if she could inform him the name of Tobit's dog. I was so much incensed at his insolence, that I should certainly have kicked him where he stood, without ceremony, had not the young lady prevented the effects of my indignation by replying, with the utmost vivacity, 'His name was Nash, and an impudent dog he was'. Nash, amidst 'universal laughter', took snuff, smiled, and passed on elsewhere.

If Smollett based this rebuttal on fact, the Beau may

have kept going until he reached Tunbridge, since in August 1748 he seems to have appeared on the Pantiles. Among other visitors was Samuel Richardson, tasting his renown on the completion of his interminable *Clarissa Harlowe*. Richardson brought back from the Wells a coloured print of its famous walk, bordered by houses with red-tile roofs, rather steep, and with gable-windows of diamond-leaded panes. The picture showed the post-office, Evans's coffee-house, and across the Pantiles, a pale-blue fence and benches under a row of trees. If Tunbridge was no longer fashionable, its attraction was dying hard, for the company on the promenade, identified in Richardson's own hand on the margin of the print, included many whom Bath would have gladly welcomed.

Amongst the visitors walked Dr Gilbert the Bishop of Salisbury, Lord Harcourt, Colley Cibber, David Garrick, the singer Mrs Fraser, Mr Pitt, the Speaker, Lord Powis, the Duchess of Norfolk, Peggy Banks, Lady Lincoln, Mr Lyttelton, the Onslows and their daughter, Loggan the artist, and William Whiston, the Cambridge divine, who was lecturing in Tunbridge on earthquakes. Richardson himself was taking the air in a costume of resplendent green. Beau Nash, in black wig, brown coat, and white stockings, did not lack illustrious companionship: he was strolling along with Mr Pitt, and between them walked Elizabeth Chudleigh, the Hon. Mrs Augustus Hervey, who, 'naked as Andromeda', had latterly attended a masque ball. Could anyone say that Nash's sun had set, even at the age of seventy-four? If the great ones no longer upheld him at Bath, he seemed yet able to collect them at Tunbridge Wells.

Nevertheless it was in Bath, in the very next year, 1749, that the Beau gained favourable mention from the foremost author of the day—Henry Fielding, who saw in Nash what Smollett had chosen to disregard. Fielding, now celebrated for his *Joseph Andrews*, and creator of Parson Adams, often came down to nearby Widcombe to visit his sister Sarah. She brought him over to Prior Park, and introduced him to Allen. Host and guest took immediate liking to each other, Fielding for his part seeing in Allen the ideal philanthropist. The author could not resist putting so open-hearted a man 'into a book', as one who constantly meditated 'in what manner he might prove himself most acceptable to his Creator by doing most good to his creatures'.

The household in Prior Park now consisted of the Allens and the Warburtons, Mrs Warburton being Allen's niece. Warburton as a rising cleric had defended Pope's *Essay on Man* from a chorus of disparagement; Pope in gratitude had presented him to Allen, who in turn gave his niece—in the year after Pope died—in marriage to Warburton. Came a day when another clergyman, young Richard Hurd, who in his preface to an edition of Horace's *Ars Poetica*, 1749, had complimented Warburton, arrived at Prior Park to *see* his friend Warburton. Hurd also there met Fielding, aged forty-two, and perceived very little good in the witch-like face of the novelist, whose nose and chin seemed trying to join. Hurd went away and summed up Fielding as 'a poor emaciated worn-out rake, whose gout and infirmities have got the better even of his buffoonery'. However, Fielding's buffoonery and infirmities, if not his gout, were at the moment enabling him to write *Tom Jones*, in which Ralph Allen was to appear as Squire Allworthy, and Beau Nash as himself.

While there is no record that Nash and Fielding actually met, nor even any precise testimony that Nash was ever entertained within the house at Prior Park, Fielding, who again and again came over to Bath from Widcombe, could hardly have missed crossing Nash's path at one time or another. At all events the novelist grew acquainted with the ways of the Beau. When in 1749 *Tom Jones* was published, Nash played a part in the chapter called 'The History of Mrs. Fitzpatrick'. That errant and reminiscing lady observed:

'And here I cannot omit expressing my gratitude to

the kindness intended me by Mr Nash, who took me one day aside, and gave me advice, which if I had followed I had been a happy woman. "Child", says he, "I am sorry to see the familiarity which subsists between you and a fellow who is altogether unworthy of you, and I am afraid will prove your ruin. As for your old stinking aunt, if it was to be no injury to you and my pretty Sophy Western (I assure you I repeat his words) I should be heartily glad that the fellow was in possession of all that belongs to her. I never advise old women: for, if they take it into their heads to go to the devil, it is no more possible than worth while to keep them from him. Innocence and youth and beauty are worthy a better fate, and I would save them from his clutches. Let me advise you therefore, dear child, never suffer this fellow to be particular with you again"'.

But Mrs Fitzpatrick had gone her own way, for 'inclination contradicted all he said', as in the case of Fanny Braddock, and indeed, Fielding may well have had that notorious episode in mind. The important thing, however, was that in his masterpiece he was saying a good word for the Master of Ceremonies at a time when the Master stood in need of it.

His decline was not without its pauses, moments when he remarkably held his own. In this year a visitor of mark was Eva Maria Weigal, a German dancer known as Mlle. Violette, who after winning approval in Vienna and Florence had in 1746 come to England. Her 'modest grace' created such a furore that she stayed, under the energetic patronage of the Earl and Countess of Burlington. Now in Bath, Mlle. Violette drew attention both by her personal beauty and by the 'delicate manner of her dress'. Lady Vane, who was the next best-dressed woman in England, admitted the charm of the dancer, and to her allowed breeding that was equivalent. The two ladies were unacquainted. But Lady Vane took the view that well-bred people 'betrayed their quality even as they passed strangers'.

Nash was asked to take Mlle. Violette out to dance a minuet. His dancing was still considered a favour. After those of precedence had danced, Mlle. Violette was therefore the first lady invited. She went through a minuet with the Master 'as void of any flourishes as it was full of grace and elegance'.

There was an anti-climax. The next lady asked to the floor, who enjoyed some reputation in Salisbury as a player of the spinet, refused to dance after Mlle. Violette. Nash thereupon saw to it that she should not dance at all, and she got no chance to demonstrate to the beaux of Bath her ear for music. In a pet the young lady returned to Salisbury and her spinet, and to her father, who was an ironmonger.

It was toward a happier event that Mlle. Violette left Bath: to marry, in this same year, David Garrick.

Not always was the Beau's conspicuous association with lady visitors so much to his advantage. The Countess of Huntingdon was now about, not harmlessly—as when on the Prince of Wales's birthday ten years earlier she had appeared in a fancy ball-gown, white, embroidered with leaves, gold shells, and vases of flowers—but as a Methodist priestess on the rampage. She was no convert of Wesley. A greater Chrysostom, George Whitefield, a man who could utter the word 'doom' with such shuddering import that fashionable men and women nearly fainted, had won her over. The Countess made Whitefield her chaplain, and set about shepherding more souls for him to save.

Selina Huntingdon was a tall widow of forty-one with a face mediaevally melancholy. She wore flowing robes, a white cloth round her shoulders, and head-dress like a prioress. Earlier engaged in politics, as one who liked to direct things and to lead people, she had turned to religion as an occupation to keep her busier still. Her shrine was in Chelsea, whither titled ladies (rather than men) repaired to confess their sins: Lady Suffolk, Lady Chesterfield, even Chesterfield's old inamorata, Lady

Fanny Shirley. And the Countess was now opening in Bath, on behalf of 'Lady Huntingdon's Connection', as her sect had grown to be called, a chapel in Harlequin Row—cynics said the address was apt—to uplift the visiting heathen. Chesterfield himself, tongue in cheek, gave the 'female Pope' £20 toward its fittings.

Nash, having been worsted by Wesley on the religious issue, changed his tactics in the case of this dominating lady, and joining other select and contrite visitors, appeared at her house, where he dutifully listened to discourses upon her favourite topic: predestination. Twenty years older than Chesterfield and a few other seemingly repentant statesmen, Nash was perhaps the hardest nut to crack.

The contrite were outnumbered in Bath by the irreverent. One such wrote verses on Nash and Lady Huntingdon, and pinned them to the walls of the Assembly-room, also to the pillars of the Pump-room. An accomplice had circulars printed, which he caused to be distributed. One of these leaflets said that the Countess, attended by a saintly sister, was to preach in the Pump-room the next morning, and that Mr Nash, to be known henceforth as the Rev. Richard Nash, was expected to preach in the evening in the Assembly-room. It was hoped that the audience would be numerous, as a collection was intended for the Master of Ceremonies, retiring from office.

The Countess said nothing. But Nash was incensed. He had incurred defeat both in opposing evangelism and in countenancing it. Abruptly he broke off his calls at Lady Huntingdon's house.

When in November Mrs Montagu came to Bath for one of her periodic and incisive surveys of its company, she touched upon such recurrent evidence of the decline of the Beau in a characteristic letter to the Duchess of Portland: 'I have not seen our friend Kit Lansdell; I hear he is disconsolate from the loss of the widow . . . But the conqueror, Mr. Gore, has carried her to Bath; by marrying so many men she has acquired a masculine spirit, and the other day distinguished herself by dispossessing a lady of her place at the play; the company at Bath did not approve of the violence of her proceedings, and if the monarch Nash had not lost most of his power and prestige, I imagine he would have obliged her to behave better'.

CHAPTER SIXTEEN

NASH AND THE NOVELISTS

NEAR Bath, at Bathford, stood Shockerwick, another landmark of the handiwork of John Wood. In his typical style, it was a house of six Corinthian columns, with wings, but with a sub-wing added to the left wing. Wood had also laid out the grounds, with rare shrubs, walks, drives, and statuary. Shockerwick commanded views as far and wide as those of Prior Park, and even the house rivalled Prior Park. But it had been built from a fortune garnered more questionably than the wealth of Ralph Allen, for Shockerwick was the abode of Walter Wiltshire, proprietor of the Assembly-room.

Nevertheless a man who with such a house could compete with Prior Park might also make some pretension as a host, and Allen himself was nothing loath to accept the hospitality of Wiltshire, nor was Henry Fielding. Nash, never a familiar figure at Prior Park, naturally took his ease at Shockerwick as a colleague of Wiltshire, even if an unfortunate one. But a man always welcome at both places, like Fielding, was William Hoare, the painter, now turned forty, and in his prime. After long study in Italy, France, and Holland, Hoare had come home to find in Bath a lucrative spot for portraits. One of the coterie at Prior Park, he had already painted Allen, Pope, Pitt, and Chesterfield. Nash had engaged him to draw in crayon the 'beauties of the day' with which to adorn the house in St. John's Court. But now Nash himself was sitting to Hoare in the drawing-room of Shockerwick.

There was no little irony in Wiltshire's fractional requiting of the Beau in this fashion.

The portrait that emerged was all that one might expect in point of finery. Nash was resplendent in his white beaver, tilted to touch his right eyebrow, in his short black wig, in his open waistcoat edged with lace, and in his brown coat swung back, and heavily frogged. All his life in Bath he was a figure in white-black-brown. The fleshy face was not so reassuring. His double chin sagged upon his stock. Hammocks under the eyes betrayed scores of years of indulgence. But the painter was perhaps most telling, not to say unkind, in the deep creases he drew at the ends of the Beau's mouth. Nash looked his age. The portrait was a one-third length, for Hoare unfortunately could not draw hands.

If the Master of Ceremonies did not look too happy in this likeness, it should be said that since the suppression of the profitable game of E O he had not found much to be happy about. Some of the more venturesome visitors persisted in running a wheel in secret. 'Whisk and the noble game of E O', confided Mrs Montagu in 1749, 'employ the evening'. But the risk of detection remained considerable. In January 1750 the Mayor and his officers raided a house in Westgate, and burnt an E O table. Peeresses had once enjoyed the privilege of keeping a gambling-house, and if in need of cash they often did. Now they faced apprehension for it.

Subdued as Bath was, it was not too deflated for a return visit in July of the Prince and Princess of Wales, who brought with them their daughter, Augusta. While Nash no doubt greeted these royal patrons of his brighter days, it is symptomatic of his relegation that he appears to have taken no part in their round of entertainment. From their landau, bringing up at the end of Market Place, the royal guests were carried in sedan chairs to the South Parade. They took tea not with Nash, but with Ralph Allen at Prior Park. Thence they proceeded to the Kingsmead Theatre to see, 'at the command of Lady

Augusta', a performance of *Tamerlane*. Nor was it apparently by any arrangement of Nash that the Prince and Princess on another day embarked in wherries for Saltford, to dine in public under tents in a meadow. Frederick gave the rustics two hogsheads of beer, whilst all the time a band played. He was a thoughtful Prince, and at least mindful of the obelisk set up to him by the Beau.

If Nash had been fit to embrace all his opportunities at this time, he would probably have arranged for the Prince to open a new theatre in Orchard Street, and have turned the performance to the benefit of the Hospital. Work on this theatre had been delayed by the death of Hippisley in 1748. John Palmer, a brewer and chandler, took over its completion. But Nash was too borne down with his years to expedite its fulfilment, and the opening (with *Henry IV*, Part I) did not occur until October.

Inasmuch as increased activity in the theatre at Bath tended to offset the curtailed freedom in gambling, the lure of the resort remained fairly constant. Bath continued to be a capital of gossip, as shown not only in the letters of Mrs Montagu and Lady Suffolk, but in more elaborate detail by the chronicles of Smollett. In 1751 he published *Peregrine Pickle*. Its suggestion was that any comely young man who visited the waters encountered adventures more than enough:

'When Peregrine, in consequence of having danced with one of the minors over-night, visited her in the morning, the Platonists immediately laid hold of the occasion, tasked their imagination, associated ideas, and with sage insinuations retailed a thousand circumstances of the interview . . . They observed that if girls were determined to behave with such indiscretion they must lay their accounts with incurring the censure of the world; that she in question was old enough to act more circumspectly; and wondered that her mother would permit any young fellow to approach the chamber while her daughter was naked in bed.

'As for the servants peeping through the keyhole, to be

sure it was an unlucky accident; but people ought to be on their guard against such curiosity, and give their domestics no cause to employ their penetration. These, and other reflections, were occasionally whispered as secrets among those who were known to be communicative, so that, in a few hours, it became the general topic of discourse; and as it had been divulged under injunctions of secrecy, it was almost impossible to trace the scandal to its origin, because every person concerned must have promulgated her own breach of trust in discovering her author of the report'.

But it was the doctors whom Smollett really set out to vilify, and, as Nash may well have reflected, the novelist considerably improved upon the diatribe by Dr Radcliffe against Bath in 1705. Peregrine took a look at the manoeuvres of the profession round the waters:

'He perceived that among the secret agents of scandal none were so busy as the physicians, a class of animals who live in this place like so many ravens hovering about a carcass, and even ply for employment, like scullers at Hungerford Stairs. The greatest part of them have correspondents in London, who make it their business to enquire into the history, character, and distemper of everyone that repairs to Bath . . . and if they cannot procure interest to recommend their medical friends to these patients before they set out, they at least furnish them with a previous account of what they could collect, that their correspondents may use this intelligence for their own advantage. By these means, and the assistance of flattery and assurance, they often insinuate themselves into the acquaintance of strangers, and, by consulting their dispositions, become necessary and subservient to their prevailing passions. By their connection with apothecaries and nurses, they are informed of all the private occurrences in each family, and therefore enabled to gratify the rancour of malice, arouse the spleen of peevish indisposition, and entertain the eagerness of impertinent curiosity'.

Yet Smollett was not so obsessed with denouncing his fellow-physicians that he failed to notice other personages in Bath. In this year of 1751 the colony of permanent residents was enriched by the addition of the actor James Quin, who at fifty-eight came to live in Bath in lively retirement. Quin was the great Falstaff of his day. For ten years he had extorted from the management of Covent Garden £1,000 annually, the highest salary ever earned by an actor, lest he desert to Garrick at Drury Lane. Now he had the sense to quit London and enjoy life in his own epicurean style. He had a sensuous face, plump, with thick lips and a fat nose, and with not too much expression until he spoke. But as Smollett later observed, Quin 'gave vent to every whimsical idea as it rose'—even as Falstaff himself—and under the stimulus of 'six good bottles of claret' he astonished the taverns of Bath with the brilliancy of his thoughts and the force he gave to them. Joking about his own fastidiousness in food and drink, he freely invited others to confirm his tastes, to the end of promoting conviviality as the happiest side of existence.

It was no wonder that Quin soon found this mode of life in Bath rather a drain upon his comfortable savings, in particular since those to whom he paid his bills began in every quarter to charge him exorbitantly. Quin complained to Nash.

'Bath', responded the Master, 'is the cheapest place in England for a man of taste'.

Quin protested that even his tastes were not so expensive as the tavern-keepers made out. But Nash, in dealing with a man of wit, was, notwithstanding his advanced years, ready with wit of his own.

'They treated you', he resumed, 'with true Christian spirit'.

'How so?' persisted the actor.

'You were a stranger, and they took you in'.

Nash in this season welcomed friends new and old alike. Even at seventy-seven he found sociability no less agreeable. In the autumn Chesterfield brought his son, now nineteen, and back from the Grand Tour, to receive from the company at Bath some needed burnishing under the eye of the Earl. The Queensberrys were there, and the Pitts. All were content to play in the Rooms at whist, in which gambling within limits was still legal, and if the Beau sadly missed the opulence of his former days, he took all the diversion he could get from the company assembled. And if he read any new books, he could hardly have failed in December to notice with satisfaction that Fielding, in contrast to Smollett, said in his dedication of *Amelia* to Ralph Allen: 'There is scarcely, as I remember, a single stroke of satire aimed at any one person throughout the whole'.

It was easy for visitors to comment upon the decrepitude of Nash as a personage; but things kept happening to sustain his reputation. In 1752 young Thomas Linley of Wells, who had studied music in Bath, settled in Bath as a singing-master, and as a conductor of the concerts. But he shrewdly determined in the main to manage, and to conduct only in default of someone better. Almost at once Linley began to invite to Bath eminent musicians and composers, to whom he yielded the baton. The superiority of the music at Bath, compared to that at other resorts, was immediately remarked, with the result that Nash as Master of Ceremonies, although having made no exertion whatever beyond sanctioning the appointment of Linley, found himself receiving tributes from all sides for the quality of his orchestra.

It was accordingly a propitious moment for a fresh visit from that odd character, the Princess Amelia. She came for the season, and comfortably settled herself in at Prior Park. The Princess had grown fat and rubicund, and quite indifferent to what people thought; she liked gambling, horseback, strong beer, and fishing in ludicrous costume. On many a winter day, in Harrison's Walks by the Avon, she took her ease in a summer-house fitted with two fireplaces.

Twenty-four years had passed since Nash had won the friendship of Amelia by his defiance of her, when he refused to let her dance after 11 o'clock had struck. Now forty-one, she was still his friend, and she allowed him to escort her to the card-tables and play at Commerce with her. She heard that Chesterfield was expected, and wanted him also, to sit on the other side of her. As soon as the bells pealed his arrival the Princess sent a message to his house in Pierrepont Street, saying she expected the Earl to join her at play, 'that he might be sure of a warm place'. Betwixt the two eminent beaux, Amelia ensured for herself an agreeable evening, win or lose.

The Princess was kind, a steady friend, generous, and charitable: but she was still inclined to tattle, now mischievous, now insolent. She took too much snuff; she still ate her breakfast standing up, and she still went hunting dressed like a man, in a round cap and a laced coat. If in the summer-house she fell asleep behind her hook and line, it was not Beau Nash, but a fish on the end of the line that awakened her. On the last day of her long sojourn the Corporation presented her with a saccharine address, in which they complimented her upon 'her obliging behaviour and unaffected condescension'.

The actual scene in which the Princess had moved was depicted in February of this year of 1752 by Bolingbroke's sister, Henrietta, Lady Luxborough, in a letter to her friend, the poet William Shenstone, whom she wished to join her in Bath: 'We can offer you friendly conversation, friendly springs, friendly rides and walks, friendly pastures to dissipate gloomy thoughts, friendly booksellers who for five shillings for the season will furnish you with all the new books, friendly chair-men who will carry you through storm and tempest for sixpence and seldom less —for Duchesses tread the streets here unattended. We have also friendly Othellos, Falstaffs, Richard III's and Harlequins, who entertain one daily for half the price of your Garricks, Barrys and Rich's. We can also offer

Ralph Allen (1694–1774), Postmaster of Bath, host at Prior Park, and colleague of Beau Nash in building the Mineral-Water Hospital

Henry Fielding (1707–54) as drawn by his friend, William Hogarth. The novelist, who with Nash frequented Shockerwick, the house of Walter Wiltshire, introduced the Beau amiably into *Tom Jones*, and in the London press commended Nash for his administration of Bath you friendly solitude, for one can be an anchorite here without being disturbed by the question "Why?"

'Would you see the fortunate and benevolent Mr Allen, his fine house and his stone quarries? Would you see our law-giver, Mr Nash, whose white hat commands more respect and non-resistance than the crowns of some Kings? To promote society and good manners, and a coalition of parties and ranks, to suppress scandal and late hours are his views, and he succeeds rather better than his brother-monarchs generally do. Hasten then your steps, for he may be soon carried off the stage of life, as the greatest must fall to the worms' repast: yet he is newly hanging' (in his smaller house opposite the old one) 'his collection of Beauties, so as to have a space to hang up as many more future belles. His Apelles is Howard (in crayon); his Praxiteles is Howard's brother, who, though a student, designs also to exercise his art in sculpture on humble paper ceilings, which are very handsome'.

Since Nash was still in control of his eminence, and the springs were so friendly in their cure, the Master of Ceremonies could hardly have been perturbed by the publication in March of *An Essay on the External Use of Water*, ... a plan for rendering the mineral waters of Bath more safe, agreeable and efficacious'. It was by the hand of Tobias Smollett, who could not be numbered by Lady Luxborough among the friendly sights of Bath. In the first part of his essay he contended that plain water was superior to mineral water; in the second part, that unhygenic conditions at Bath endangered the health of patients: these conditions were the promiscuous bathing of the diseased, the lack of shelter in the baths from the weather, and their filthy surroundings.

But the Beau, having withstood a similar attack on the waters by Dr Radcliffe so many years before, when the reputation of the new Master was only in the making, took no notice, now that his reputation, as well as that of the spa, was secure. He knew Smollett well enough, and knew what lay behind his charges. The novelist was a disappointed doctor. Having taken his medical degree at Aberdeen in 1750, he had been trying to establish himself at Bath, where the medical life and all its quackery fascinated him. However sound his knowledge, however justifiable his onslaught in *Peregrine* upon the physicians, enabling their patients to make fun of them, these same patients thought Smollett not serious enough for Bath. But there were personal objections to this pale blue-eyed Scot with his long pointed nose: his temper was irritable, and he failed to make himself pleasing to the ladies. David Hume said that although Smollett was full of human kindness within, he was like a coco-nut outside. Nor was his radical essay, designed to get him a practice at the waters, destined to enhance his standing. Nobody was coming to Bath either to drink plain water or to bathe in it.

No doubt there were some who denounced Smollett for calling the whole medical profession fools and quacks, and yet, within a month after he had published his Essay, in April, he could point in Bath to a distinguished case of foolishness amongst them. William Cheselden, the famous anatomist, known afar for his operation for the stone, came to Bath, drank ale after eating hot buns, disregarded the advice of a fellow-doctor to take an emetic, and succumbed.

Nash himself was feeling not too well, and in August he went down to his allied resort of Tunbridge for a change. On 12 August he startled the ladies by falling in what they called 'a fit'. Mrs Montagu, who now divided her holidays between the two spas, informed her husband on the next day: 'Mr Nash had a fit yesterday, by which it is imagined this monarch will soon resign that Empire over mankind which in so extraordinary a manner he gained and has preserved'. A little more sympathetic was Lady Jane Coke, writing on the same day to Mrs Eyre: 'Poor Nash has had a fit, but does not seem to mind it, though he looks just a-going'. However, it was a rhymer of the hour who gave vent to the general anxiety:

> Say, must the friend of human kind,
> Of most refined, of most diffusive mind,
> Must Nash himself, beneath these ailments grieve?
> He felt for all—he felt—but to relieve,
> To heal the sick, the wounded to restore,
> And bid desponding Nature mourn no more . . .
> O let not death with hasty strides advance;
> Thou, mildest Charity, avert the lance;
> His threatening power, celestial maid, defeat,
> Nor take him with thee to thy well-known seat;
> Leave him on earth some longer date behind,
> To bless, to polish, and relieve mankind.
> Come thou, kind health! O quickly come away,
> Bid Nash revive, and all the world be gay.

There were some in both Tunbridge and Bath who might have said that if the Beau could survive this doggerel he could survive anything. However, on his return to Bath later in the month he did find, health or no health, fair incentive to 'revive'. A few local residents, including members of the Corporation, having thought fit to honour Beau Nash with a full-length statue in marble from the hand of William Hoare the painter, a statue in the costume which had made the Beau the cynosure of the Assembly, were about to set up this memorial in the Pump-room.

The Pump-room had grown into a kind of gallery of sculpture, a hall of fame. Local authorities, proud of the repeated visits paid Bath by the eminent, adorned this rendezvous with busts and statuary of the eminent, in order to remind less accomplished guests of the exalted company, past and present, whose resort they shared. Although Nash had for some years looked down from an oil portrait, full length itself, upon the throng here imbibing, he was now to be elevated into marble. Perhaps the councillors responsible for hanging that portrait carried something on their conscience, a matter they were ambitious to neutralize. Acting unwittingly, unless they had fancied the juxtaposition of a scientist, a beau, and a poet would form an effective contrast, they had flanked the tall painting of Nash in his finery with busts of Pope and Sir Isaac Newton. Upon this incongruity a man of nimble pen, probably Chesterfield, had leapt:

> Immortal Newton never spoke
> More truth than here you'll find,
> Nor Pope himself e'er penned a joke
> Severer on mankind.
>
> The picture placed the busts between
> Adds to the satire strength;
> Wisdom and wit are little seen,
> But folly at full length.

If indeed the Earl was the author, one is tempted to speculate upon what he would have written if Nash had asked him, instead of Pope, to contribute the inscription for the obelisk in honour of the Prince of Wales—except that, in those years, Chesterfield in politics was being rather careful.

And now, in 1752, 'folly at full length' was to make a renewed appearance in the Pump-room, this time in the more sober medium of three dimensions, high, white, and awesome, in a niche all its own, beyond the gibes of the scoffers. No difficulty had arisen over the expense: gifts on account of the memorial had been received from 'several of the principal inhabitants'.

When the day came round for the unveiling, a day in mid-August, another humorist, but a man who chanced to be the greatest novelist of the age, Henry Fielding, was in Bath to lend his applause. He chose to go beyond an epigram.

While Fielding's own important work as a novelist was done, he had for a year or more in London been absorbed in public service, and the chance that arose in Bath to take part in an act of homage attracted him. Always friendly to Nash, and cognizant of his unique achievement, Fielding now sent a note to the *Covent Garden Journal* for 24 August saying that this statue of Nash represented 'gratitude for his well-known prudent management for above forty years, with regard to the regulation of the diversions, the accommodations of persons resorting hither, and the general good of the city'.

CHAPTER SEVENTEEN

OCTOGENARIAN

A GENTLEMAN of Vauxhall sent in April 1753 a request in verse to a gentleman at Bath, asking his friend to tell him

> How grand the balls, how fine the place,
> How gay and splendid shines his grace
> How Nash, diversions all his care,
> Affects of youth the sprightly air.

To the minds of many admirers far and near the Beau was immortal. Nash himself of course had said he was like Nestor, a man of three generations—the Beau of his youth, the Beau of his manhood, and the Beau of his old age. The Princess of Wales, as if in memory of her husband lately dead, presented to the Master an agate etui mounted in gold, with a diamond to open it, and another diamond upon its top. (The Princess Amelia, proportionately beneficient, had given him the silver tureen.) Nor did Nash altogether relinquish his own show of patronage, especially if he could thereby gain something for his cherished Hospital. In October he joined the Duchess of Queensberry ('Kitty') and Lady Suffolk as patrons at a performance in the Assembly-rooms by the 'Bath Company of Comedians'. With curtain at six o'clock, and with prices from a shilling for a seat to three shillings for a box, they raised forty pounds.

By remaining perennially in Bath the Master retained some of his noble friends; if he had forsaken his career at the waters and moved to London, it is unlikely even they, upon the whole, would have recognised him. While he had been highly successful in 'democratising' Bath, he had no control over the behaviour of his visitors after they left, and the fact that the 'uppers and lowers' danced together at the Assembly meant nothing at all outside the boundaries of Bath. In this year the irascible Smollett, who could never write a book without taking a pot-shot at the town, or at Nash and all his works, published *Ferdinand Count Fathom*, in which narrative Fathom had this to say:

'A maxim ... universally prevails among the English people, namely to overlook and wholly neglect, on their return to the metropolis, all the connections they have chanced to acquire during their residence at any of the medical wells. And this social disposition is so scrupulously maintained, that two persons who lived in the most intimate correspondence at Bath or Tunbridge shall, in four and twenty hours, so totally forget their friendship, as to meet in St. James's Park without betraying the least token of recognition, so that one would imagine those mineral waters were so many streams issuing from the river Lethe, so famed of old for washing out all traces of memory and recollection'.

The fact that young men and young women of uncertain position who had risen socially whilst at Bath were disillusioned upon their return to town only confirmed the power of Nash in his own domain. Nor did his great age in years witness in the Assembly-rooms any weakening of this levelling rule amongst the dancers. Nash himself waned in power only from his infirmity. His real friends, of whatever standing, remained staunch, acknowledging his monument to be not only the social ordering of Bath, but its amazing embellishment as carried out by John Wood.

This overworking architect, exerting himself far beyond his strength, yet seemingly incapable of rest, now in 1754 laid out Gay Street, to run from the northeast side of Queen Square to the Circus, itself a circle of thirty-eight palatial houses displaying all three of the Greek styles. The first stone-laying occurred on 7 February. The Circus, some 300 feet across, was to contain a statue of the elderly King on a horse, while in addition to Gay Street, two other boulevards, fifty-two feet wide, were to lead away from the centre, and terminate each with a building to correspond in design. But the master-builder, though barely fifty years old, did not live to see this plan fulfilled. Never robust, almost frail, he died 'in harness' after only a few more stones of the Circus had been added to the first. The triumvirate of the makers of Bath was broken. However, Wood's son and namesake undertook to realise all of his father's intentions, and even to carry out more of his own.

Of the two survivors, Ralph Allen was rich, and Beau Nash was poor. The Master in his prime had started countless 'public subscriptions' for the benefit not only of the community, but of individuals as needy as he himself was now. Toward the end of this year, therefore, his friends set afoot a collection to help him. It was to be not ostensibly a charity, but a fund returnable in copies of a book, a *History of Bath and Tunbridge for these last forty years, by Richard Nash, Esquire, with an apology for the Author's Life.*

In December the Corporation set the example by subscribing for twenty-five copies. A lady 'celebrated for her wit and accomplishments, who was lately married to a foreign gentleman', and by that sign did not mind being identified, wrote an appeal, which in part ran in this wise:

> All ye, to Nash, whom these gay realms obey
> Who fifty years hath borne undoubted sway,
> And ne'er one tax imposed, subscriptions pay.
>
> Come, every graceful Beau, and gentle Belle,
> Subscribe your names, in praise of bagatelle;
> And every fop, in honour of your train,
> That one fop lives who hath not lived in vain . . .
>
> Deists, who, calling all religion odd,
> Beauty and order substitute for God,
> Nash and his writings with fit reverence view;
> Beauty and Order none, like Nash, e'er knew.

> Whilst ye, of upright faith and sober sense,
> Behold in him the hand of Providence,
> Health to the sick, the wounded limb restore,
> Supply the wants of age, and friendless poor.
>
> Statesmen, who sleepless pass the midnight hour,
> See Nash, without a thought, support his power;
> See all, with one consent, his word revere,
> No oath to blind, no law to raise a tear.
>
> Mirror of Princes, hail! thy life may show,
> To Kings enthroned, what Kings shall never know,
> To rule without a rival, or a foe.

Nash, alas, was for his own part no writer, not even about himself. If he could not write during the years of his vigour, it was hardly to be expected that he should be able to turn author when past the age of eighty. To all appearances he was sincere in his declaration to produce the book; yet there were doubtless many who subscribed for it without ever intending to demand their money back if the book did not appear. On the other hand, one Sarah Scott, in a letter in November to Mrs Montagu, took an uncharitable view of the arrangement:

'The whole money, two guineas, is to be paid down at once, for he does not pretend any book is come out. Some have subscribed ten guineas, some five, and a good many hundreds of pounds are already subscribed. It is to be kept open for life, and people give to him who will not part with a guinea to relieve the greatest real and unmerited distress imaginable. The pretence is that he has but little more than £200 a year, which is not supposed true, but if it was, surely it is full equal to his merits, whether one considers them as moral or entertaining. To such ladies as have secret histories belonging to them, he hints he knows every one's private life and shall publish it'.

Mrs Scott was evidently unaware of Nash's own time-honoured philanthropy; as well, she overlooked the little circumstance that, since the price of one copy of the book was two guineas, those who subscribed five guineas could hardly be paying for two and a half copies, and were therefore making part, if not all, of their contribution a gift.

This money kept the Beau afloat. What was more, he doughtily refused to yield up his stewardship. Such was the talk in London of his longevity that at White's Lord Mountford betted Sir John Bland that Nash would outlive Colley Cibber, the everlasting comedian who in this year of 1755 was eighty-four. (Mountford, had he himself lived, would have won; but before the year was out both he and Bland committed suicide.)

Nash survived even Simpson of the Assembly-rooms, who died in May. With the approval of the Master, Simpson's son succeeded him, although the theatre in Bath, instead of its two companies, one in the Assembly-rooms and the other in Kingsmead, now became a monopoly in the hands of John Palmer. Upon such rearrangements Nash could still exercise his managerial genius.

But he had lost his fertility of inventing new modes of entertainment. Buffeted by the winds of changing fashion, he could not change with them. He looked back. He took immense pride, still, in settling the style of a lady's cap, or in assigning to a lady her proper place in a country dance. So long had the Monarch pursued these trivialities, so long had he overseen them with the utmost punctiliousness, that his set mind now occupied itself with little else. He did not relish the prospect that people might stop calling him an 'odd fellow'.

By day the old Beau sat in the coffee-houses, telling stories in which himself played the principal character. Sometimes he repeated the same string of stories on the same day. If anyone spoke of a German war, or of Elizabeth Canning the imposter (lately examined by Henry Fielding and transported for perjury), Nash broke in with:

'I'll tell you something to that purpose, which I fancy will make you laugh'. Then he went on with a yarn that was completely irrelevant; but he 'laced it with an oath, asserveration and grimace', to make it go. His favourite story at these interludes ran thus:

'A covetous old parson, as rich as the Devil, scraped a fresh acquaintance with me several years ago at Bath. I knew him (possibly James Lake, commoner at Jesus) when he and I were students at Oxford, where we both studied damnationly hard; but that's neither here nor there. Well. Very well. I entertained him at my house in John's Court (no, my house in John's Court was not built then); but I entertained him with all that the city could afford, the rooms, the music, and everything in the world. Upon his leaving Bath, he pressed me very hard to return the visit, and desired me to let him have the pleasure of seeing me at his house in Devonshire.

'About six months after, I happened to be in that neighbourhood, and was resolved to see my old friend, from whom I expected a very warm reception. Well: I knocks at his door, when an old queer creature of a maid came to the door and denied him. I suspected, however, that he was at home, and going into the parlour, what should I see, but the Parson's legs up the chimney, where he had thrust himself to avoid entertaining me. This was very well.

'My dear, says I to the maid, it is very cold, extreme cold indeed, and I am afraid I have got a touch of my ague. Light me the fire if you please. La, sir, says the maid, who was a modest creature to be sure, the chimney smokes monstrously. You could not bear the room for three minutes together. By the greatest good luck there was a bundle of straw in the hearth, and I called for a candle. Well, good woman, says I, since you won't light me a fire, I'll light one for myself, and in a moment the straw was all in a blaze. This quickly unkennelled the old fox. There he stood in an old rusty nightgown, blessing himself, and looking like—a-hem—egad'.

His listeners forgave him much. There were those amongst them who remembered that Beau Nash was the first to foster a taste for 'elegant' amusements, first to promote an ease of demeanour in people who were notorious for their dislike of sociability, their reticence, their awkward bearing. He reformed them. These people had carried back to London and elsewhere the lesson that Nash had taught them, and in consequence England had in his own lifetime grown more congenial in its character and more gregarious in its ways.

Nor was the doddering Master in his hours of retreat from the coffee-houses and the Assembly-rooms suffered to be alone. His quondam mistress Juliana Papjoy, from whom he had parted because of lack of funds to provide for her, returned to him to attend to his wants. No longer on horseback, no longer riding through the streets of Bath as 'Lady Betty Besom', she yet found compassion for the man of her heyday. The change from mistress to nurse was not too hard, except that Juliana at times had to be imperious, and summon a doctor even when Nash forbade her so doing. Since the jovial Cheyne had died the Beau had no more use for doctors than for preachers—though John Wesley came in this autumn, 1755, to dine at Prior Park, whilst in Southgate Street George Whitefield was harrowing the sinners.

Indeed Nash continually baffled those who seemed to take a sort of ghoulish comfort from his infirmities. Far from being tethered in his house by Juliana, he was off in September to Tunbridge, as if he had as much to do with running its wells as he had ever done. And there, at least, it seemed that age could not wither his reputation as a Samaritan. One William Henderson, a Quaker, straightway sought the aid of the Beau on behalf of 'Mr. Annesley', reputed by Henderson to be the legitimate son and heir of the late Lord Baron of Altham, of whose estates, in Anglesey, Henderson had been the agent. The Quaker had known Annesley since he was six years old. The rest of the family, however, refuted the young man's claim, and turned him off penniless. Henderson now entreated Nash, in his time-honoured capacity of philanthropist, to assist the waif by a subscription.

It says much for the old Master that even in his own pinched circumstances he gave ear to this appeal. Tunbridge was now outside his 'province'. Nevertheless he set going a collection for Annesley on the spot. While it did not prosper like his subscriptions of old, he assured Henderson that if he would send the defrauded young man to Bath in the season of the following year, Henderson would then see 'how much Nash would be Annesley's friend'. Enough funds would be assured to enable the heir to contest his inheritance.

Enemies of the Beau would have said that he postponed dealing with this case in order to get rid of it. In fact he meant to do exactly as he said, and even with his authority in decay to start the appeal in Bath differing in no respect from scores of others he had launched in his palmy days. He seldom considered 'the merit or the industry of the petitioner'. To undertake any charity, he wished only to be convinced of the misery which it was to relieve.

Henderson took Nash at his word, sent Annesley to Bath in October 1756, and wrote to Nash to remind him of his promise. The Quaker was a persuasive phrasemaker. He reminded the Beau of the 'everlasting honour' which would reward his services, and now that Nash was 'in the vale of life' would 'crown all his good actions'. The subscription was 'to extricate for a distressed young nobleman an immense estate from the hands of oppression' and to do this would 'fix a ray of glory on Nash's memory'.

All this wheedling was more than enough to set the aged but flattered listener to work. Embarrassed by poverty though he was, Nash headed the list of subscribers himself. The petition must have reminded him of his golden days of collecting for his Hospital, and now, even at eighty-two, with all the dregs of his energy he threw himself into a kind of counterpart of his old campaigning. It would be difficult to say whether the response to his call, enough response to lengthen the list to a sizable sum, came more out of pity for Annesley or for Nash.

Sad to relate, this money 'for the relief of indigence' went instead to 'a set of reptiles'. As for the estates in Anglesey, poor Nash had not reckoned upon the opposition. The property never came into the hands of the heir, who, too feeble to fight his own battles, had entrusted the combat to a noncombatant Quaker—or so it seemed.

The end of this sorry business left the Beau in rather a crumpled state. It was the last subscription he attempted, for if donors could not be sure that the money collected by him would be used for the purpose submitted, their confidence in the collector as a judge of charities, however innocent he himself might be of misappropriation of funds, no longer held firm. Nash kept more and more aloof from the Assembly-rooms. He stayed mostly in his house, with his Juliana.

In September 1757 arrived Mrs Delany, for the purpose of 'going to the Bath balls'. As a wife she was a woman of some ability, for having married Patrick Delany of Trinity College, Dublin, she had within a year of their wedding got him chosen Dean of Down. Long in the neck, plump of face, with rather protuberant but kindly eyes, she let her abundant curling hair fall to her shoulders, and in the ball-room she was an arresting figure by very force of her personality. But she found Bath singularly quiet, if not desolate, in the absence of its stricken Master. 'No Nash', she complained to her sister Anne Dewes, 'no music in the Pump-room!'

Mrs Delany was looking in the wrong place for the old Beau. She might perchance have found him in Morgan's coffee-house, telling stories of himself to whoever would listen, stories perhaps of his feats of strength in his college days, in his Temple days in London. 'Here I stand, gentlemen, that could once leap forty-two feet upon level ground, at three standing jumps, backward or forward, one, two, three, dart like an arrow out of a bow.

But I am old now. I remember I once leaped for three hundred guineas with Count Klopstock, the great leaper, leaping-master to the Prince of Passau . . . and went beyond him one foot three inches and three-quarters, measured, upon my soul . . .'

CHAPTER EIGHTEEN

THE FINAL PAGEANT

THOMAS Gainsborough, aged thirty, arrived in Bath in 1758, to practise his art. He was a lean alert sharp-featured young man, with eyes rather severely sharp, a long sharp nose, and sharply arched brows. In due course he rented a house for fifty pounds a year, an ornate house in the Circus, faced with three layers of columns, doubled. These layers seemed to embrace the whole of Greek architecture, the ground-floor being Doric, the first floor Ionic, and the second Corinthian, while above all ran a parapet topped with decorated vases. Here was John Wood in his most clamourous vein. And from this house Gainsborough announced that he would paint portraits for five guineas.

One of his first sitters, in its studio-drawing-room, is said to have been Nash. The artist, generous but capricious, and easily irritated, was spirited in conversation and quick at repartee. He and Nash at all events understood each other. Gainsborough worked at great speed, sometimes using brushes as long as a javelin, fully six feet.

If he did not actually paint the Beau, he missed so few of the other celebrities in Bath that he soon raised his fee to eight guineas. Then he boldly put it forth that he would paint half-lengths for fifty guineas, and full lengths for a hundred. Equally diligent was Gainsborough at landscapes, which he preferred to do; but landscapes, less in the fashion, were not so vendible.

Soon he was confronted by James Quin, the epicure of venison, turtle, and claret. Quin must have his portrait done, too. But Gainsborough did not like risking his brushes upon actors, having failed with both Garrick and Samuel Foote. 'Rot 'em for a couple of rogues!' he exclaimed. 'They have everybody's faces but their own'.

Yet Gainsborough yielded to the gout-ridden Quin, with whom he liked to fence in bouts of irascibility—as with Nash, in fact. Quin came crawling to the painting-room, and tapping:

'Is old Grumpus at home?'

'Well', Gainsborough railed as he opened the door, 'and how is toe?' If the painter was finishing a landscape, he was gay: if doing a portrait he growled.

Quin offered criticism. 'Sometimes, Tom Gainsborough', he wheezed, 'the same portrait, from your rigmarole style, appears to my optics the veriest daub—and then, the devil's in you, and I think you're a Van Dyck'.

Everybody at Bath was afraid of Quin except Gainsborough and Nash, and even Nash had occasionally been 'hugged by the bear'.

The meeting of the Beau with Gainsborough was Nash's last enlivening acquaintance, and it did him a world of good. If a measure of rejuvenation was possible to a man of eighty-four, he got it from the brisk painter. The old Master of Ceremonies, in whom fortitude did not run strong, shuddered at the thought of death. Never admitting that his end was approaching, he daily insisted that he was in full health, even as he made his way about in a wheel-chair which itself was not devoid of creaking.

He sold his rings, his watches, his pictures. The Corporation, taking pity, and cognizant of their manifold benefits from him in the past, voted the Beau in 1760 ten pounds a month for the rest of his days. It was barely enough, there in the little house in Saw Close where he lived, to allow Juliana Papjoy to minister to his immediate wants.

From a window in this house, which at least boasted an impressive decorated doorway giving the lie to the

James Quin (1693–1766). At Covent Garden his performance in *Henry IV* as Falstaff surpassed the acting of Garrick as Hotspur. Quin in 1757 retired to Bath and befriended Nash in his last years

The Abbey Church. Scene of the burial of Beau Nash, in his 88th year, in February, 1762

poverty within, Nash could look ruefully across the street to the great mansion in St. John's Court which he had vacated, and observe its new tenant, the plump-faced Mrs Delany, coming out and going in. She kept a diary. 'This morning', she noted, on an October day, of Nash's new painter-friend, 'went with Lady Westmorland to see Mr. Gainsborough's pictures. They may be called what Mr. Webb unjustly says of Rubens—they are "splendid impositions".'

But it was this same Mrs Delany who reported that the Beau, almost to the very end, stubbornly refused to yield up his authority. House-bound more and more, he seldom got into the Assembly-rooms; but when he did, in his wheel-chair, he still umpired disputes with the tenacity for which he was famous. An acting Master of Ceremonies, one Collett, who had by this time replaced Nash for most purposes, deferred to the King of Bath when the occasion arose. Collett was a man whose pleasing manners won him the approval of the women; but his opposition to gambling made him otherwise an unwelcome substitute for the old Master. Although the younger man was a graceful dancer, a clever 'quick-change' mimic, and a skilful player at shuttlecock, these acquirements were hardly enough to qualify him in the eye of the generality of visitors, and Collett still had a task to make his place secure.

It was on 28 October 1760 that Mrs Delany wrote to Mrs Dewes of an incident in point. A Mr Sloper was in Bath with Mrs Cibber, when upon a certain evening a nubile daughter of this liaison suffered embarrassment at the Assembly. 'Mr. Sloper', Mrs. Delany reviewed the scene, 'who is here with Madame Cibber and a daughter by her (a young woman) had been much offended that his daughter was not taken out to dance; she was, the first night; and a sensible clever woman whose daughter was taken out after her refused to let *her* dance; this put a stop to Miss Cibber's being asked again; and on Sunday night, in the midst of the room, Mr. Sloper collared poor

Collett, abusing him at the same time, and asking if he had been the occasion of the affront put upon his daughter; he (Collett) said it was "by Mr. Nash's direction"—the poor wretch (Nash) is now wheeled into the Room; Mr. Sloper had some discourse with him, and so the matter ended'.

While it is not chronicled that it was also by Nash's direction, in this same year, that subscriptions were simultaneously opened for 'prayers at the Abbey' and for gambling, the coincidence was one that he might well have instigated in his earlier years. At the end of the first day's collections, the score stood in 67 to 12 favour of 'gaming at the Rooms'. Soon afterward a local rhymer had his say:

> The Church and Rooms the other day
> Opened their books for prayer and play;
> The priest got twelve, Hoyle sixty-seven:
> How great the odds for Hell 'gainst Heaven!

The pulse of the day, that is, with Bath ten times as popular as when the Beau had first taken charge, beat against the stringency of Collett, and in favour of the 'sporting' policy so long countenanced by his great predecessor.

Nash was outliving all his contemporaries, even the old King, who had just died (25 October), nine years junior to the Beau, at seventy-seven. With the accession of George III, the Monarch of Bath could be said to have lived under seven reigns. Quin, speaking reminiscently of Nash and his equipage to the young King's uncle, the Duke of Cumberland (now retired from the Army), alluded to 'Old Neddy and his nags'. But not to all visitors at the spa was the Beau, relic that he was, a deplorable sight. One Mr Angelo described him as 'the finest old gentleman he had ever seen'. 'He reminds me', said Angelo, 'of the oldest of the old French regime'.

Yet this winter was his last, and he did not quite live through it. Richard Nash died submissively in his little house in Saw Close on 3 February 1761, aged eighty-seven.

THE FINAL PAGEANT

It would have pleased the Monarch whom nothing but death could utterly dethrone to know that a grateful Corporation, on the day after, voted fifty pounds for a burial befitting him. Nash himself could not have ordered the procession—which took place on the fourth day, at five o'clock in the afternoon—more amply to satisfy his sense of the requisites. He was to be escorted from his house to the Abbey Church in all the pomp with which he had so often escorted Royalty into Bath.

There was not much of the winter daylight left; and that, too, seemed properly suggestive. At the head of the cortège walked pairs of charity girls. Then came the boys, from the charity school, who sang a dirge in quatrains. The 'city music' followed, and to reinforce it, at intervals, Nash's own band, which he had time out of mind laboured to make worthy of Bath. Three clergymen, not one, marched after it—gentlemen who had toiled in the Beau's lifetime to instil in him the ways of repentance. The pall, next in line, and laden with sable plumes, was borne by the six senior Aldermen. Then as chief mourners came the masters of the Assembly-rooms—as well they might, for who in those rooms could replace Beau Nash? The final representative officers were the beadles of that Hospital which was Nash's most enduring monument, that building for which he had more diligently and relentlessly collected the funds than any other man. Last in line walked the poorer patients themselves, cripples included, for whom the Master of Ceremonies had done so much; they were witnesses that when all was said he had been not a mere attendant upon personages.

No throng that ever gazed upon a mediaeval pageant could have exceeded in numbers the crowd who watched this procession, even from roofs, and who heard, above the marching music, 'the muffled bells ringing a peal of Bob Major'.

It was the end of an epoch, just at nightfall, as the doors of the Abbey Church closed upon the mourners.

'And now, pray', said old Briggs irreverently (in Fanny

Burney's *Cecilia*), 'how does he cut up? What has he left behind him? A twey-case, I suppose, and a bit of a hat won't go on a man's head'. (A twey-case was a pocket-case, mounted and oblong, for a mirror and tweezers.)

In fact Nash, having sold nearly all of his possessions in order to live, had left not much more. It is said that he gave his medals to the Bodleian, the library of his university. (The Bodleian has no record of them.) He had kept some of his pictures, and his few books, including the poems of the little man who wrote that inscription for Frederick's obelisk. Only three of his trinkets, each with a strong personal identity, had the old Beau refused to part with. One was a jewelled box from his most exalted guest, the Prince of Wales. Another was the etui, from Frederick's widow, the agate etui, mounted in gold, ornamented with those two diamonds. The third trinket, a gold box, bore no royal association, but may have carried with it a touch of romance in respect of one of two ladies: it was a gift from the Countess of Burlington, patroness of Mlle. Violette, and its lid was adorned with a miniature of Lady Euston.

If the Bathonian Monarch died thus poor in possessions, he died rich in praise. Two of his local admirers and supporters, Dr Oliver and Dr King, wrote long tributes to Nash (about 150 and 100 lines) which recounted rather repetitively his many well-known qualities, his achievements, and some of his faults. King called his words an epitaph; it required a slab of marble that dwarfed most of the memorials, themselves far too long, in the Abbey Church. But had Nash not been the 'Supreme Being' of the community?

Dr Oliver entitled his lines 'a faint sketch of the life, character, and manners' of the Beau. Nash had come to Bath because his mind was 'superior' to both the Army and law. In celebrating his hero, the Doctor displayed no 'faint' turn for antithesis: 'those of the highest rank became his subjects, while he became the servant of the poor'. One fresh point the panegyrist did make: that

Nash was unique in being an absolute monarch who was never cruel. Nor was the 'sketch' entirely favourable. Nash's 'fire', not having been restrained in youth, brought him too often into flaming acts, ill-judged. And he had been generous, as everyone knew, to the point of imprudence. In the end, the Beau had paid 'the tax of weakness and infirmities for multiplicity of days'.

While King wrote more elegantly, in Latin, he found equal difficulty in saying anything not generally known for many years to most of the visitors to Bath. Unlike Oliver, however, he alluded to Tunbridge, which he described as Nash's 'celebrated province'. One acute touch was that the white hat of the Master signalised the candour of his mind. It was also quite in order for King to submit that it was Nash (not John Wood) who 'adorned Bath with beautiful structures'—inasmuch as those buildings would have been unlikely to rise had the Beau not presided for a lifetime over the spa. And the faults of the Master of Ceremonies, in King's opinion, were so harmless that if not estimable they were pardonable. In bestowing the laurels of antithesis, King was not far behind Oliver. 'He found out', wrote Dr King, 'the happy secret of uniting the vulgar and the great, the poor and the rich, the learned and the ignorant, the cowardly and the brave, in the bonds of society'. This truth, if long recognised, really bore repeating, for it was Richard Nash's contribution to his age, if not to the ages. Only one questionable suggestion, in all the hundred lines of this epitaph, stood out: that Kings and governors should imitate Nash's example. (They have infinitely more varied and abundant human wickedness to contend with.)

Of the multitude of minor 'character-writers' who aspired to distinguish themselves by obituaries, one soared to a climax that earned for him, a year later, satirical mention from Oliver Goldsmith. The character-writer declared of Nash that 'impotent posterity would in vain fumble to produce his fellow'.

However, less than a generation thereafter, posterity had so far reasserted its potency as to produce Beau Brummell. That dandy, of course, had not risen to the figure in London that he became, but for the example in Bath set him by Beau Nash.

NOTES

AUTHORITY for material facts and quotations will be found hereunder; when not stated, the source (at the approximate date of the context) is Goldsmith's *Life of Richard Nash, of Bath, Esq.*, 1762. The characterisation of various personages, unless otherwise noted, is either from DNB or from contemporary paintings. To other works oftenest consulted the following initials apply:

W. *An Essay Towards a Description of Bath.* John Wood. 1749.
B. *Life and Letters at Bath in the 18th Century.* A. Barbeau. 1905.
M. *Bath Under Beau Nash*, L. S. Benjamin ('Lewis Melville'). 1907.

For special aid generously given on Nash's early life I have to thank Mr W. C. Rogers, historian of Swansea; Mr J. F. Jones, Curator of the County Museum, Carmarthen; and Mr J. N. D. Baker, Bursar of Jesus College, Oxford. For information on Nash in Tunbridge Wells I am much indebted to Sir William Wigham Richardson, Bt., of Calverley Park; and to Mrs Durell and Miss Malden, of the Tunbridge Wells Library and Museum. Acknowledgement is likewise due to the Director of the Victoria Art Gallery, Bath; the staff of the Public Library, Bath; and to the staff of the London Library, for their kind assistance.

CHAPTER I

The Poyers and the Nashes: R. Fenton, *Hist. Tour through Pembrokeshire*, 1903, 132 ff., 293-4; G. N. Wright, *Hist. Guide to Bath*, 1864, 286; *Y Cymmrodor*, XXVII, 158 (Llewellyn Williams).

Man, Nash, and the Poyers in Swansea: Rogers, *vid. sup.*

The 'glasseworke' and its equipment: Original documents on Swansea, Royal Institution of South Wales, Folio Vol. 1870, p. 45.

Nash fined: Common Hall Books, Swansea, 1673-4.

Mathew, Hannah and Catherine Poyer: Register, Swansea Parish Church. Christening of Richard Nash: do.

John Man as Collector of the Port: Letters of Elizabeth Gywnn to her husband Richard, the 'Patent Customer' of South Wales; Rogers, *vid. sup.*

The house in Goat Street (pulled down about 1820): do.

Queen Elizabeth Grammar School: engravings, *Carmarthenshire Antiquarian Society*, (Transactions), IV: 12, 16. Pupils in Nash's time, and Maddocks as Master at Abergwilly: do, II: 201. John Maddocks: Foster, *Alumni Oxoniensis*; *Carm. Ant. Soc.* (Transactions), XXV: 11; XXVI, 4. The Headmaster's house: do, IV; 12, 16.

Jesus College in Nash's time: *Victoria Hist. of the Counties of England*, Oxfordshire, 264-79, *passim*; C. E. Mallet, *Hist. of Oxford*, II: 194. Jonathan Edwards: E. G. Hardy, *Jesus College*, 149.

Admission of Nash and his college-mates: University Matriculation Books, Bodl. Lib., and Buttery Books, Jesus Coll. Their battels: the Buttery Books. James Lake: Baker, *vid sup.*

Nash's life in Oxford: *Goldsmith's Works*, ed. Gibbs, 1885, 56; *Bentley's Miscellany*, II, 414-25, 'Memoir of Beau Nash'; W. Russell, *Eccentric Personages*, 118-19; G. N. Wright, *op. cit.*, 286.

CHAPTER II

Nash in the Army: Wright, *vid. sup.*; *Chambers's Journal*, 15 Oct. 1859. As a Templar: J. Tunstall, *Rambles about Bath*, 182; Bentley, *op. cit.*, do; J. March, *Bath Celebrities*, 85; Wright, *op. cit.*, 286; *Gentleman's Magazine*, 1762, p. 487. As a philanthropist: *Spectator*, 248 (14 Dec. 1711). Treasurer to the Benchers: Russell, *op. cit.*, 119.

Highwayman of Hounslow Heath: *Y Cymmrodor*, XXVII, 158. Nash's twenty love-letters: M. 16. The cabman: *Jests of Beau Nash*, 1763, 25.

CHAPTER III

Queen Anne and Prince George at Bath: W. 324.

Bath under Webster: B. 14; M. 37, 41; J. Doran, *Memories of our Great Towns*, 83; J. Earle, *Bath*, 1864, 177; J. March, *op. cit.*, 82 ff.

The town-hall: R. Warner, *Hist. of Bath*, 1801, 219. How Bath looked to Nash at thirty: M. 84.

Bath in 1700: J. Ashton, *Social Life under Queen Anne*, 108–12. *A Step to the Bath*, anon., *passim*. Headdress of the Ladies: P. Thicknesse, *The Valetudinarian's Guide*, 1780, 55.

Nash as aide to Webster: M. 41–2. Webster killed: W. Lyte, *Bath in the 18th Century*, 50.

CHAPTER IV

Abolishing swords: *Blackwood's Magazine*, July 1840, 'The Monarch of Bath', 773–92; Thicknesse, *op. cit.*, 66. Nash at the baths: Thicknesse, do, 55 ff. The new band: M. 43–4. Inspection of lodgings; Willard Connely, *Brawny Wycherley*, 1930, 308.

Radcliffe on Bath: *A Letter from a Citizen* (from his 'shop') *of Bath to Dr. Radcliffe—at Tunbridge, passim*. Nash on Radcliffe: W. 222–3. The 'play-room': B. S. Penley, *The Bath Stage*, 1892, 17 ff.

Wycherley on Bath in March: W. Connely, *op. cit.*, 280, 282, 306 ff. The new pavilion and the pageant: M. 46–7.

Price to Harley: *Hist. MSS. Comm.*, XV, App. IV, 329. Nash on streets and roads: W. 224–5; M. 46. Charges at Pump-room and Assembly-house: W. 417, 437–8.

Nash the original wearer of a white hat: *Life of James Quin*, anon., 1887, 58. His dress in winter, and his wen: do.

CHAPTER V

Journey from London down the Bath Road: J. Doran, *op. cit.*, 80 ff.

Nash catching the highwaymen: W. Lyte, *op. cit.*, 17 ff. How he democratised Bath: W. 411. The inns of Bath: M. 76–7; *Jests, op. cit.* 55.

The gravity of the minuet: B. 60–1 (illus.) Nash the Philosophic Beau: George Meredith, *A Tale of Chloe*, 13. Defoe: quoted by B., 169.

Swift to Stella: *Journal*, 24 Aug. 1711. Addison on Bath: *Spectator* No. 179. Lady Orkney to Lady Oxford: *Hist. MSS. Comm.*, Portland, V, 90. Cromwell on Wycherley: W. Connely, *op. cit.*, 314–5.

Ogling in Abbey Church: J. Doran, *op. cit.*, 90.

John Gay: Willard Connely, *Sir Richard Steele*, 186–7; his letter to Parnell: quoted by M., 178.

CHAPTER VI

Tunbridge Wells in 1714: J. Macky, *A Journey Through England*, I, 56. (Nash made no habit of visiting Tunbridge until some years later.)

Allen finds the shipment of arms: B. 244. Visitors in Bath: W. 227.

Allen and Wade: M. 94; E. Sitwell, *Bath*, 1932, 187–8.

NOTES

Lady Eliz. Hastings and the Mineral-Water Hospital: W. 275, 286. Subscriptions first invited: M. 262-3, quoting W. Purchases of Humphrey Thayer: W. 227.

Lady Cowper to the Duchess of Marlborough (unpublished): Blenheim MSS. Duchess to Lady Cowper: M. 160. The Duke at piquet: *Spence's Anecdotes*, IV, 123. The Duchess on Books: M. 183.

'Court Tales': quoted by B., 37-8, 40. Nash the 'Governor of Bath': *Hist. MSS. Comm.*, Stuart, II, Sir J. Erskine to the Marquis de Villefranche, 11 Oct. 1716. Nash and the Women: *Universal Magazine*, Nov. 1862. Fanny Murray: *Notes and Queries*, Series II, Vol. IV, 1, 41. Nash no whoremonger: *Jests, op. cit.*, 47.

Nash's house: W. 231; Tyte, *op. cit.*, 38; J. F. Meehan, *Famous Houses of Bath*, 1901, 42-3. Mrs Lindsey: *Tunbrigalia*, 1719.

Killigrew, Assembly-Rooms, Weymouth House: W. 228, 319. Nash at home: *Bentley, vid. sup.*, 420; Thicknesse, *op. cit.*, 13.

CHAPTER VII

Bath *versus* Continental spas: *Blackwood, vid. sup.*, 789. 'The Pleasures of Bath', anon. pamphlet, BM.

Lady Bristol: Hervey, *Letter-Books*, II, 161, Aug. 14, 19, 1721. Mrs Bradshaw to Mrs Howard: *Letters of Henrietta, Countess of Suffolk*, I, 73-6. Lady Bristol; Hervey, *op. cit.*, Aug. 30, Sept. 9, 20; B. 96; M. 153 fn. Nash on Mrs Bradshaw: Suffolk, *op. cit.*, I, 79. Duchess of Queensbury: B. 31; *Complete Peerage*; Tyte, *op. cit.*, 17.

Congreve at Bath: B. 168. Nash and Dr Cheyne: *Jests, vid. sup.*, 2; M. 246-7. Character of Cheyne: March, *op. cit.*, 122.

Defoe on Bath: *Tour Thro' Gt. Britain*, ed. of 1722, quoted by M., 189-90. Nash in 1723: 'Characters ... at Bath in October, 1723', anon., 1724. (Dedicated to Nash).

Bell Causey: H. R. Knipe, *Tunbridge Wells and Neighbourhood*, 1916, 13 ff; Margaret Barton, *Tunbridge Wells*, 1937, 200.

Nash as jester: *Universal Magazine, vid. sup.* Lady Bristol: Hervey, *op. cit.*, 1722. The hospital subscriptions: W. 275-8. Allen's contribution: March, *op. cit.*, 95. Nash in Bristol: Hervey, *op. cit.*, Sept. 14, 18.

CHAPTER VIII

Nash and the bridegroom: Wright, *op. cit.*, 291. Fortune-hunting at Bath: *Blackwood, vid. sup.*, 784.

Molly Lepel to Mrs Howard: Suffolk, *op. cit.*, I, 181-4.

Improvements by Allen and Wade: Sitwell, *op. cit.*, 188. Cheyne's weight, diet, and authorship: *Hervey's Memoirs*, ed. Sedgwick, 1931, xviii, 969.

Fanny Braddock: M. 194-6, 199 fn. Her suitor: *Gentleman's Magazine*, 1762, 487.

CHAPTER IX

Wood in Yorkshire and London: W. 232. He settles in Bath: do, 242; M. 89. Portrait of Wood: Tyte, *op. cit.*, who published this portrait, does not certify its authenticity. His first buildings: B. 283-4; M. 87-90.

Princess Amelia: Tyte, *op. cit.*, 38; M. 62, 85, S. 95. Lord Boyle on Amelia at Tunbridge: *Orrery Papers*, I, 81. Nash's ultimatum to her: B. 33. Her gift to Nash: Tyte, *op. cit.*, 24.

Allen's house, Lilliput Alley: M. 94; Sitwell, *op. cit.*, 189-90. Lady Anne Irwin to Lord Carlisle: *Hist. MSS. Comm.*, XV, App. VI, 61. The ancient excavations: W. 242-4. Thayer's ballroom opened: M. 116.

The return of Fanny Braddock: M. 196. Progress on the Hospital: W. 286.

The end of Fanny: *Gentleman's Magazine*, Sept. 1731, 'On the Unhappy Self-Murder of Miss Fanny Braddock at Bath'. Her brother's comment: Horace Walpole, *Letters*, ed. Toynbee, III, 334.

CHAPTER X

The young Duke of Bolton: B. 37; Goldsmith's *Nash*, ed. Cunningham, 1854, 61. Orrery on Nash: *Hist. MSS. Comm.*, Dartmouth I, Report XI, App. V, 327. Orrery to Kempe: *Orrery Papers*, I, 81 ff. Books dedicated to Nash: quoted in *Bentley, vid. sup.*, 421.

Nash's aspiration in Tunbridge, 1732: Knipe, *op. cit.*, 13. Opposition of Mrs Causey: do. The new Pump-room in Bath: W. 270; Tyte, *op. cit.* 17 ff.

Verses to Amelia: *A Description of Bath*, anon., BM.

Nash and the linen-draper: R. Graves, *A Spiritual Quixote*, 1772, 81. Standing of the Beau in the mid-1730's: *Bentley, vid. sup.*, 420.

The Prince of Orange at Bath: Willard Connely, *The True Chesterfield*, 1939, 142. Hervey on the Prince: quoted by Tyte, *op. cit.*, 24.

CHAPTER XI

Arrival of Chesterfield: W. Connely, do. 145. The company: Lady Suffolk, *op. cit.*, II, 114–19. Chesterfield on Nash: do.

Death of Harrison: W. 319. Mrs Hayes succeeds him: R. E. M. Peach, *Life and Times of Ralph Allen*, 215; J. Tunstall, *Rambles about Bath*, 1847, 221.

Death of Bell Causey: Knipe, *op. cit.*, 16. Nash takes charge: Barton, *op. cit.*, 202; M. 217. Sarah Porter: Knipe, do; Barton, do, 206–7. (According to Knipe, Mrs Porter outlived Nash himself by a few months, dying in 1762).

Progress of John Wood: J. Earle, *op. cit.*, 216.

Fanny Murray and Kitty Fisher: *N. & Q.*, II, IV, 1, 41. Lord Hardwicke saw this picture, a little later, at Mrs Montague's in Cambridgeshire. Another portrait of Kitty Fisher, alone, is in the library at Petworth, Sussex. For Fanny Murray in 1746–48–63, *vid.* Horace Walpole, *Letters*, ed. Toynbee, ii 213 n. 346; v 394.

'The Diseases of Bath', anon., 1737. BM. Death of Mrs Lindsey: W. 319. Catherine Lovelace succeeds: Peach, *op. cit.*, 215.

Suppression of the theatres: M. 119, 263.

Verses to Nash at Tunbridge: *Tunbrigalia* for 1737–39.

Arrival of the Chesterfields: W. Connely, *op. cit.*, 160–1. Chesterfield to Lady Suffolk: *Suffolk Letters*, II, 161. The Earl watching a minuet: Meehan, *op. cit.*, 29.

Nash to the fashionable lady: G. Meredith, *op. cit.*, 24.

CHAPTER XII

Beginnings of Prior Park: B. 246. Nash to London: W. 290. He revives the theatres: Penley, *op. cit.*, 17 ff.

Bear Inn and Lock's Lane: J. Tunstall, *op. cit.*, 179. The stone-laying of the Hospital: W. 290; M. 263; Wright, *op. cit.*, 131. Arrival of Chesterfield: W. Connely, *op. cit.*, 166–7. Frederick in Bath: do; Tyte, *op. cit.*, 24. Gift of the Prince to Bath: *London Magazine*, 13 July 1845.

CHAPTER XIII

The haunted house: Meehan, *op. cit.*, 119. Wesley at Bath: R. Southey, *Life of Wesley*, I, 324 (ed. 1925); B. 155. Nash augments his band: *The Spiritual Quixote, vid. sup.*, 170. Charles Wesley: Southey, *vid. sup.* See also Wesley's *Journal*, May 1739.

NOTES 179

The Prince and Princess of Wales at Tunbridge: T. B. Burr, *Hist. of Tunbridge Wells*, 1766. 112 ff.

Miss Robinson at Bath: E. J. Climenson, *Elizabeth Montagu, Queen of the Blue-Stockings*, 2 vols., 1906. See also Rebecca West, 'Elizabeth Montagu', in *From Anne to Victoria*, 1937, 164-187.

Nash and the beggars: C. G. Harper, *The Bath Road*, 1899, 210. The gambling games: Wright, *op. cit.*, 291; Tunstall, *op. cit.*, 231; B. 38.

Juliana Papjoy: Peach, *op. cit.*, 215 ff; *Gentleman's Magazine*, April, 1777. M. 266-71, combines these views with vv. by W. G. Benham.

Arrival of Princess Mary: Tyte, *op. cit.*, 25. The fire: do.

The leaders in the Hospital: Wright, *op. cit.*, 131. Wood begins the North Parade: Tunstall, *op. cit.*, 74. Nash and E O: do, 231; B. 38; Peach, *op. cit.*, *passim*; Blackwood, *vid. sup.*, 783.

Quatrain on Nash: B. 44.

CHAPTER XIV

Opening of Prior Park: B. 283; Wright, *op. cit.*, 377; P. Thicknesse, *New Prose Bath Guide*, 1778, 77; J. F. Watson, *Life of Warburton*, 1863, 240; J. Earle, *op. cit.*, 216.

Mrs Holden's gift: W. 294. Allen elected Mayor: M. 94. Accommodations in the Hospital: J. Earle, *op. cit.*, 216; W., *passim*; the rules, do, 249-50.

Chesterfield to Cheyne: W. Connely, *op. cit.*, 198-9. Dr Burton on Nash: quoted by J. F. Watson, *op. cit.*, 240, in Burton's Latin: 'magister ineptiorum, effoetus et edentulus senex', whose face was 'ferrugineus ardor, et sine verecundia rubor immutabilis'. On Allen: do.

Nash's Tunbridge manager: It is surprising that the efficient Sarah Porter had not given her Master, Nash, some inkling of the peculations, or at least of the faulty book-keeping, in the gaming-room.

Death of Lord Hawley: *Complete Peerage*. Lady Hawley: B. 59.

Effects of the Act of 1745: *Gentleman's Magazine*, 1762, 487; Blackwood, *vid. sup.*, 783; M. 228. Nash's appearance: B. 44, quoting the *London Magazine*, *vid. sup.*

Mrs Montagu at Tunbridge Wells: B. 81; W. C. Sidney, *England in the 18th Century*, 1891, II, 51. Nash in Saw Close: Peach, *op. cit.*, 215 ff.

CHAPTER XV

Princess Caroline: Horace Walpole, *op. cit.*, II, 183. Princess Margaret: do, II, 231. Nash's Coronation Day Ball: *Hist. MSS. Comm.*, Astley, 355. John Hippisley: Tyte, *op. cit.*, 105; Penley, *op. cit.*, 17 ff.

Concert breakfasts: 'Description of Bath', *vid. sup.* The pauper charity: Earle, *op. cit.*, 216. Nash 'embezzling': M. 222, quoting the *Bath Journal*. Eliz. Chudleigh at the ball: W. Connely, *op. cit.*, 420. Miss Barton, *op. cit.*, 3-4, suggests that since by 1748 Samuel Johnson had received no doctorate, the 'Dr. Johnson' in Richardson's drawing was James Johnson, D.D. (1742). This Johnson (1705-74) became in 1748 canon of St. Paul's and chaplain to the King. The 'Mrs. Johnson' in the drawing, so called in 18th century terminology, then appears to have been a spinster sister, who for many years favoured Tunbridge Wells as a resort.

Hurd on Fielding: M. 96. Nash and Mlle. Violette: Thicknesse, *Memoirs and Anecdotes*, 1788, II, 217. Nash and Lady Huntingdon: B. 157; *Life and Times of Selina, Lady Huntingdon*, 1844, I, 445. Whitefield: W. Connely, *op. cit.*, 277-8, 387, 394. Chesterfield and Lady H.: B. 159.

Mrs Montagu to Duchess: *Hist. MSS. Comm.*, Marquis of Bath, I, 331.

CHAPTER XVI

Nash at Shockerwick: Meehan. *op. cit.*, 43. Hoare in Bath: B. 287.
Mrs Montagu on E O: to Anne Donnellan, *vid.* Climenson, this date. The raid: Tyte, *op. cit.*, 54. Return of the Prince and Princess of Wales: do, 24; Penley, *op. cit.*, 17 ff.
Opening of the theatre in Orchard St.: B. 66–7; Penley, do; W. Arrival of Quin: B. 199 fn. Quin as an epicure: H. Angelo, *Reminiscences*, 1830, I, 170. On Bath: Meehan, *op. cit.*, 90; R. Warner, *Literary Recollections*, 1830, II, 2.
Princess Amelia returns: W. Connely, *op. cit.*, 338–9. Lady Luxborough to Shenstone: Tyte, *op. cit.*, 127. Smollett in Bath: *Life*, R. Anderson, 1806, 35–6; *Life*, D. Hannay, 1887, iii, B. 171. Death of Cheselden; *Gentleman's Magazine*, April 1752.
Nash's fit at Tunbridge: *Letters of Lady Jane Coke to Mrs. Eyre*, 1747–58, ed. Mrs Rathbone, 1899, Aug. 12, 1752. The verses: M. 226–7.

CHAPTER XVII

Nash like Nestor: Bentley, *vid sup.*, 423. The Princess's etui as gift: Tyte, *op. cit.*, 24. Nash as patron to the Comedians: Penley, *op. cit.*, 23. Death of John Wood and succession of his son: B. 284.
Verses on the subscription to Nash's 'History': *Jests, op. cit.*, 81. Sarah Scott to Mrs Montagu: Climenson, *op. cit.*, 17 Nov. 1754.
Simpson and Palmer: Penley, do, 27. Identity of the parson with James Lake: *vid. sup.*, Chap. II. Nash as promoter of 'elegant' amusements: Bentley, *vid. sup.*, 425. Return of Juliana Papjoy: Peach, *op. cit.*, 228.
Whitefield in Southgate St.: Tyte. *op. cit.*, 106. Nash in Tunbridge in Sept.: for a description of Tunbridge in 1756, *vid.* Thackeray, *The Virginians*, Chap. XXXIV, 320.
Mrs Delany to her sister (Anne Granville): *Autobiography and Correspondence*, ed. Lady Llanover, Sept. 1756.

CHAPTER XVIII

Arrival of Gainsborough: B. 288–90. Rates for portraits: do. His house: Meehan, *op. cit.*, 17. It is Meehan who states that Gainsborough painted Nash (at 84); but Meehan gives no authority for his assertion, nor is such a portrait elsewhere mentioned.
Nash, Quin and Gainsborough: H. Angelo, *op. cit.*, 170–1. Gainsborough on Garrick and Foote: Thicknesse, *Life of Gainsborough*, 1788, 54. Gainsborough's method of painting: W. Connely, *op. cit.*, 444.
Nash's pretensions to good health: Bentley, *vid. sup*, 422. His pension from the Corporation: Town Council Minutes, Bath, 1760. Mrs Delany on Gainsborough: *Autobiography*, Oct. 1760, *vid. sup.* In Nash's house: Meehan, *op. cit.*, 43.
Character of Collett: Wright, *op. cit.*, 298; B. 112. Mrs Delany on Sloper and Collett: *Correspondence, vid. sup.*, 28 Oct.
Subscription for prayers at the Abbey, 1760: W. C. Sidney, *op. cit.*, II, 62. The rhyme about the subscription: *Gent. Mag.*, quoted by B., 58. Quin on Nash: H. Angelo, *op. cit.*, I, 171. Angelo's father on Nash: do.
Start of the funeral procession: *Gentleman's Magazine*, 1762, 487. The peal of Bob Major: Bentley, *vid. sup.*, 422, quoting a newspaper of Bath on the procession. *Cecilia*: published 20 years later; the character of Nash was perhaps the more vivid in the mind of the young authoress in consequence of her friendship with Mrs Delany.

INDEX

Addison, Joseph, 42, 43, 44
Aesop, by Vanbrugh, 16-19
Allen, Ralph, 54-5, 59, 74, 82, 89, 92, 111, 113, 122, 126, 129, 130, 131, 133, 141, 146, 147, 151, 159
Ambery Mead, Bath, 87
Amelia, Princess, 88-9, 98, 151, 157
Anne, Queen, 21, 23
Annesley, 163-5

Badminton, 22
Banks, Peggy, 140
Bath Company of Comedians, 138, 157
Bath, discovered by Society, 21; Nash arrives, 24; is appointed Master of Ceremonies, 27; the most fashionable watering-place, 34; fortune hunters descend, 45; literary prestige, 52; improvements in the town, 61; John Wood's architectural embellishments, 86-90, 126; the new Assembly Rooms, North and South Parades, Queen Square, 87-8, 90; the 'Constructive Triumvirate', 90; Queen Square completed, 105; theatre opened in Kingsmead Street, 112; a law against gambling, 124; new games to circumvent the law, 124, 126; E O brings new life to the spa, 128; opening of Hospital, 130; law against gambling tightened, 135
Bath Journal, 139
Bath Road, the, 37-8
Bath Unmasked, The, by Odingsells, 80, 138
Bear Inn, Bath, 38, 112
Beaufort Castle, Swansea, 4, 22
Beaufort, Dukes of, 4, 22, 32
Berenger, Mrs, 67
Berkeley, George, 51
Bladud, 31
Blenheim Castle, 106, 111
Blount, Martha, 51, 103
Bodleian, The, Oxford, 172
Bolingbroke, Lord, 103, 133
Bolton, Duke of, 94
Boursault, Edmé, 16

Boyle, Lord, 88
Braddock, Fanny, 84, 91, 92, 93, 104, 142
Braddock, Lt. Edward, 84, 93
Braddock, Major-General, Edward, 84
Bradshaw, Peggy, 65-7
Bristol, Countess of, 65, 66, 67, 68-9, 72-4, 75
Brummell, Beau, 174
Bryan, Nash's footman, 78, 97
Buckley, Mrs, 109
Burlington, Lady, 103, 142, 172
Burney, Fanny, 172
Burton, John (Giant Jack), 133, 134

Canning, Elizabeth, 161
Carleton, Lord, 67
Carlisle, Lord, 90
Carmarthen, 4, 5
Causey, Bell, 71, 98, 104, 105
Chandler, Mary, 101, 109
Cheselden, William, 154
Chesterfield, Lord, 102, 103, 107, 109, 110, 114, 122, 123, 131, 133, 137, 144, 151, 152, 156
Chesterfield, Lady, 143
Cheyne, Dr, 69, 83, 92, 106, 107, 131, 133-4, 163
Chudleigh, Elizabeth, 140
Cibber, Colley, 17, 19, 140, 161
Cibber, Mrs, and daughter, 169
Clarendon, Earl of, 67
Clarissa Harlowe, 140
Coke, Lady Jane, 154
Collett, Acting Master in place of Nash, 169
Congreve, William, 66-7
Conscious Lovers, The, by Steele, 79
Cook, inventor of E O game, 126-7, 131, 136
Coombe Down, 111, 129, 133
Cooper, Lady, 56
Court Tales, 57, 60
Cumberland, Duke of, 170

Defoe, Daniel, 42, 70
Delany, Mrs, 165, 169
de Querouaille, Louise, 23

181

Dodington, Bubb, 114
Drury Lane Theatre, 67
Dryden, John, 9

Edwards, Jonathan, Principal of Jesus College, Oxford, 7
E O (Even and Odd), 126–8, 131, 134, 135, 147
Esope à la Ville, by Boursault, 16
Essay on Criticism, 44, 49
Essex, Earl of, 86
Etherege, Sir George, 9
Euston, Lady, 172
Evan's Coffee-House, Tunbridge Wells, 140

Ferdinand, Count Fathom, by Smollett, 158
Fielding, Henry, 140–1, 151, 156, 161
Fisher, Kitty, actress, 106
Foote, Samuel, 168
Fraser, Mrs, 140
Frederick, Prince of Wales, 114–15, 121, 147

Gainsborough, Thomas, 167–9
Garrick, David, 140, 143, 168
Gascoigne, Richard, 51
Gay, John, 51, 52, 66–7, 68, 122
Gay, Dr Robert, 86, 92
Gentleman's Magazine, verses in praise of Nash, 132
Germaine, Sir John, 32
Gilbert, Dr, Bishop of Salisbury, 140
Goldsmith, Oliver, 173
Gore, Lord, 32
Grantham, Lord, 32, 73
Granville, Lord, 32
Greenway, Thomas, 60
Guardian, 46, 49, 55

Harcourt, Lord, 140
Harley, Robert, 32, 42
Harrison, Thomas, 33, 61, 104
Harrison's, 65, 69, 74, 78, 80, 82, 90, 104
Hastings, Lady Elizabeth, 55
Hawley, Lord, 128, 134
Hawley, Lady, 128, 132, 134, 136
Hayes, Elizabeth, (later Lady Hawley), 104, 107, 128
Health and Long Life, by Dr Cheyne, 83
Hervey, Lord, 83, 100
Hervey, Lady, 81, 83
Hetling House, 125
Highwaymen, 38–9
Hill, John, 6, 8
Hill, Lewis, 6
Hippisley, John, 80, 138, 148
Hoare, William, 146–7, 155

Holden, Mrs Jane, 130
Holder, Elizabeth (the second Mrs Ralph Allen), 89, 129
Hospital, the General, 55, 74, 83, 87, 92, 107–8, 112, 115, 126, 130–1, 132, 138
Hume, David, 154
Huntingdon, Selina, Countess of, 143
Hurd, Richard, 141
Hyde, Lord, 32
Hyde, Lady Kitty (afterwards Duchess of Queensberry), 67

Irwin, Lady Anne, 90

Jenkins, Sir Leoline, 6, 7
Jesus College, Oxford, 5–10
Jones, Dean David, 57
Jones, H., 5
Jones, William, Archdeacon of Carmarthen, 4
Joye (and see Cook), 127, 131, 136

Kaye, Lady, 95
Kempe, Bath Councillor, 95
Kendall, Duchess of, 81
Killigrew, William, 61
King, Dr, 173
Kingsmead Square, Bath, 106
Klopstock, Count, 166

Lake, James, 6, 8, 162
Lansdowne Hill, Bath, 32–3, 39
Lepel, Molly (Lady Hervey), 81, 83
Lilliput Alley, Bath, 89, 111
Lincoln, Lady, 140
Lindsey's, 65, 73, 103, 104, 107, 124
Lindsey, Mrs, 60, 87, 90, 91, 104, 107
Locke, John, 20
Lock's Lane, Bath, 112
London Magazine, 109
Lovelace, Catherine, 107, 124
Lunn, Sally, 89
Luxborough, Lady, 152–3
Lyttelton, Mr, 114, 140

Maddocks, John, Headmaster of the Grammar School, Carmarthen, 5
Marlborough, Duke and Duchess of, 49, 56–7, 67, 75–6, 106, 113
Montague, Lady Mary Wortley, 67
Montagu, Mrs (formerly Elizabeth Robinson), 135, 144, 147, 148, 154
Morgan's Coffee-House, 69, 75, 83, 165
Mountford, Lord, 161
Murray, Fanny, 59, 60, 106, 124

Nash, John, 4
Nash, Point, Swansea, 4

INDEX

Nash, Richard, father of Beau, 1–4, 6, 8, 9, 11, 22
Nash, Richard (Beau), born at Swansea, 3; at school, 4; at Jesus College, Oxford, 6, 8–10, 162; an ensign, 11; tries the law, 12; dubbed 'the Count', 13; Master of the Revels, 13; offered a knighthood, 14; rejected by Miss Verdun, 16; as gambler, 19–21; goes to Bath, 21; Assistant Master of Ceremonies, 24; elected Master, 27; prohibits wearing of swords, 28; improves lodging accommodation, 29; bottles Spa Waters, 30; opens Pump-room, 31; draws up a code of laws, 34–6; dancing and decorum, 41–2; has thoughts of Tunbridge Wells, 53; and the Hospital, 55, 74, 83, 87, 92, 107, 112, 115, 126, 130, 131, 132, 138; his detractors, 57–60; his house in St. John's Court, 60, 62, 78, 125; mode of life, 62–3; at Tunbridge Wells, 65; restrains the Grantham family, 73; loses £1,400, 76; his coach, 78; plans to develop Tunbridge Wells, 97; rebuilding Baths and Pump-room, 98; a jewelled snuff-box from Prince of Orange, 100; Master of Ceremonies at Tunbridge Wells, 104; orders an obelisk to be put up in Queen Square, 116; his care for the poor and workless, 123; sues his gaming partners, 134; goes to live in Saw Close, 136; sells snuff-boxes, 137; accused of embezzlement, 138; collapses, 154; voted a pension, 168; death, 170; funeral, 171
Nevell, Bishop, 73
Newton, Sir Isaac, his bust at the Pump-room, 155–6
Norfolk, Duke of, 32, 109
Norfolk, Duchess of, 109, 140

Odingsells, Gabriel, 80, 138
Oliver, Dr William, 92, 126, 130, 131, 172
Orange, Prince of, 100, 103
Orchard Street Theatre, 137–8, 148
Orkney, Lady, 43, 74
Orrery, Lord, 95
Oxford, 5, 6–10, 162
Oxford, Lady, 43

Palmer, John, 148, 161
Pantiles, The, 54, 97, 105, 121, 140
Papjoy, Juliana, 124, 163, 168
Parnell, Thomas, 51–2
Pauper Charity, The, 138
Pembroke, 1, 2, 5, 11

Peregrine Pickle, 148
Peterborough, Lord, 81
Phillips, Ambrose, 43
Pitt, William, 114, 140
Playhouses suppressed, 107
Pleasures of the Bath, The, 64
Pope, Alexander, 31, 44, 49–52, 103, 116, 117, 122–3, 130, 133, 141, 155
Porter, Sarah, 105, 132
Portland, Duchess of, 122, 144
Powell, David, 6
Powell, T., 5
Powis, Lord, 140
Poyer, Catherine, 2
Poyer, Colonel John, 1–2
Poyer, David, 1
Poyer, Elizabeth, 2
Poyer, Hannah, 2
Poyer, Matthew, 2
Prévost, Abbé, 102
Price, Robert, reports on Bath scene, 32, 42–3
Princess Caroline, 125, 137
Princess Margaret of Hesse, 137
Princess Mary (daughter of George II), 125
Princess Royal (wife of Prince of Orange), 100, 103
Princess of Wales, 157
Prior, Matthew, 67
Prior Park, 111, 129–30, 133, 140–1, 146, 151
Pulteney, William, 113, 114

Queensberry, Duchess of, 67, 68, 157
Queen Square, Bath, 88, 89, 105, 115
Quin, James, 150, 167, 170

Radcliffe, Dr John, 29–31, 53, 149, 153
Rape of the Lock, The, 49
Relapse, The, 16, 19
Richardson, Samuel, 122, 140
Robinson, Elizabeth, 121–3, 135 (and see Montagu, Mrs)
Roderick Random, 139

S ———, Mr, and Fanny Braddock, 84
Samborne, Richard, 75
St Albans, Duke of, 72, 74
Scarborough, 20, 21
Scott, Sarah, 160
Shenstone, William, 152
Shirley, Lady Fanny, 144
Shockerwick, 146
Shrewsbury, Duchess of, 32, 56, 66
'Simon Honeycomb', and the fortune-hunters of Bath, 45
Simpson's Rooms, formerly Harrison's, 128
Sloper, Mr, and his daughter, 169

Smollett, Tobias, 139, 148–50, 153–4, 158
Spectator, 43, 44, 46, 47
Stanhope, Charles, 103
Steele, Sir Richard, 39–40, 41, 44, 46–9, 55, 75, 79
Suffolk, Countess of, 66, 103, 109, 143, 148, 157
Swift, Jonathan, 43

Tatler, 39, 40, 41, 47, 48, 55
Thayer, Humphrey, 56, 90, 92
Thynne Family, 61
Tompion (the clockmaker), 37, 49
Tunbridge Wells, 29, 53–4, 60, 65, 70, 71, 78, 88, 97, 104, 105, 108, 121, 131, 135, 140, 163

Vanbrugh, Sir John, 16, 17
Vane, Lady, 142
Verdun, Miss, 16–19
Villiers, Barbara, 23, 36
Violette, Mlle. (see Weigal), 142–3, 172

Wade, General George, 55, 59, 74, 82, 129
Walsingham, Lady, 81, 102
Warburton, William, 141
Webster, Captain, Master of Ceremonies at Bath, 23, 24, 27
Weigal, Eva Maria (Mlle. Violette), 142–3, 172
Wesley, Charles, 119, 120
Wesley, John, 119–21, 143–4, 163
Westgate House, 73
Westmorland, Lady, 169
Whiston, William, 140
Whitefield, George, 143, 163
White Hart Inn, Bath, 38
White Lion Inn, Bath, 38
William III, 13, 14
Wiltshire, Walter, 124, 128, 132, 134, 136, 146
Wood, John, 86–90, 92, 105, 111, 126, 130, 146, 158, 159
Wycherley, William, 9, 31, 44, 50, 58

York, 20, 21